3007782144

D1806363

J

Contents

Use of guidance

THE APPROVED DOCUMENTS

This document is one of a series that has been approved and issued by the Secretary of State for the purpose of providing practical guidance with respect to the requirements of Schedule 1 to and regulation 7 of the Building Regulations 2000 (SI 2000/2531) for England and Wales. SI 2000/2531 has been amended by the Building (Amendment) Regulations 2001 (SI2001/3335).

At the back of this document is a list of all the documents that have been approved and issued by the Secretary of State for this purpose.

Approved Documents are intended to provide guidance for some of the more common building situations. However, there may well be alternative ways of achieving compliance with the requirements. Thus there is no obligation to adopt any particular solution contained in an Approved Document if you prefer to meet the relevant requirement in some other way.

Other requirements

The guidance contained in an Approved Document relates only to the particular requirements of the Regulations which the document addresses. The building work will also have to comply with the requirements of any other relevant paragraphs in Schedule 1 to the Regulations.

There are Approved Documents which give guidance on each of the Parts of Schedule 1 and on regulation 7.

LIMITATION ON REQUIREMENTS

In accordance with regulation 8, the requirements in Parts A to K and N (except for Paragraphs H2 and J6) of Schedule 1 to the Building Regulations do not require anything to be done except for the purpose of securing reasonable standards of health and safety for persons in or about buildings (and any others who may be affected by buildings or matters connected with buildings).

Paragraphs H2 and J6 are excluded from regulation 8 because they deal directly with prevention of the contamination of water. Parts L and M are excluded because they respectively address the conservation of fuel and power and access and facilities for disabled people. These matters are amongst the purposes, other than health and safety, that may be addressed by Building Regulations.

MATERIALS AND WORKMANSHIP

Any building work which is subject to the requirements imposed by Schedule 1 to the Building Regulations should, in accordance with regulation 7, be carried out with proper materials and in a workmanlike manner.

You may show that you have complied with regulation 7 in a number of ways. These include the appropriate use of a product bearing CE marking in accordance with the Construction Products Directive (89/106/EEC)[1] as amended by the CE Marking Directive (93/68/EEC)[2], or a product complying with an appropriate technical specification (as defined in those Directives), a British Standard, or an alternative national technical specification of any state which is a contracting party to the European Economic Area which, in use, is equivalent, or a product covered by a national or European certificate issued by a European Technical Approval Issuing body, and the conditions of use are in accordance with the terms of the certificate. You will find further guidance in the Approved Document supporting regulation 7 on materials and workmanship.

Independent certification schemes

There are many UK product certification schemes. Such schemes certify compliance with the requirements of a recognised document which is appropriate to the purpose for which the material is to be used. Materials which are not so certified may still conform to a relevant standard.

Many certification bodies which approve such schemes are accredited by UKAS.

Technical specifications

Under section 1(a) of the Building Act, Building Regulations may be made for various purposes including health, safety, welfare, convenience, conservation of fuel and power and prevention of contamination of water. Standards and technical approvals are relevant guidance to the extent that they relate to these considerations. However, they may also address other aspects of performance such as serviceability, or aspects, which although they relate to the purposes listed above, are not covered by the current Regulations.

When an Approved Document makes reference to a named standard, the relevant version of the standard is the one listed at the end of the publication. However, if this version has been revised or updated by the issuing standards body, the new version may be used as a source

---

[1] As implemented by the Construction Products Regulations 1991 (S.I. 1991/1620).

[2] As implemented by the Construction Products (Amendment) Regulations 1994 (S.I. 1994/3051).

of guidance provided it continues to address the relevant requirements of the Regulations.

The appropriate use of a product which complies with a European Technical Approval as defined in the Construction Products Directive will meet the relevant requirements.

The Department intends to issue periodic amendments to its Approved Documents to reflect emerging harmonised European Standards. Where a national standard is to be replaced by a European harmonised standard, there will be a co-existence period during which either standard may be referred to. At the end of the co-existence period the national standard will be withdrawn.

THE WORKPLACE (HEALTH, SAFETY AND WELFARE) REGULATIONS 1992

The Workplace (Health, Safety and Welfare) Regulations 1992 contain some requirements which affect building design. The main requirements are now covered by the Building Regulations, but for further information see- *Workplace health, safety and welfare. Workplace (Health, Safety and Welfare) Regulations 1992. Approved Code of Practice L24.* Published by HSE Books 1992 (ISBN 0 7176 0413 6).

The Workplace (Health, Safety and Welfare) Regulations 1992 apply to the common parts of flats and similar buildings if people such as cleaners and caretakers are employed to work in these common parts. Where the requirements of the Building Regulations that are covered by this Part do not apply to dwellings, the provisions may still be required in the situations described above in order to satisfy the Workplace Regulations.

The Requirements J1, J2, J3, J4, J5 and J6

This Approved Document, which takes effect on 1 April 2002, deals with the following Requirements which are contained in the Building Regulations 2000 (as amended by SI 2001/3335).

Requirement	Limits on application
Part J Combustion Appliances and Fuel Storage Systems	
Air supply	
J1. Combustion appliances shall be so installed that there is an adequate supply of air to them for combustion, to prevent over-heating and for the efficient working of any flue.	Requirements J1, J2 and J3 apply only to fixed combustion appliances (including incinerators).
Discharge of products of combustion	
J2. Combustion appliances shall have adequate provision for the discharge of products of combustion to the outside air.	
Protection of building	
J3. Combustion appliances and fluepipes shall be so installed, and fireplaces and chimneys shall be so constructed and installed, as to reduce to a reasonable level the risk of people suffering burns or the building catching fire in consequence of their use.	
Provision of information	
J4. Where a hearth, fireplace, flue or chimney is provided or extended, a durable notice containing information on the performance capabilities of the hearth, fireplace, flue or chimney shall be affixed in a suitable place in the building for the purpose of enabling combustion appliances to be safely installed.	
Protection of liquid fuel storage systems	
J5. Liquid fuel storage systems and the pipes connecting them to combustion appliances shall be so constructed and separated from buildings and the boundary of the premises as to reduce to a reasonable level the risk of the fuel igniting in the event of fire in adjacent buildings or premises.	Requirement J5 applies only to- (a) fixed oil storage tanks with capacities greater than 90 litres and connecting pipes; and (b) fixed liquefied petroleum gas storage installations with capacities greater than 150 litres and connecting pipes, which are located outside the building and which serve fixed combustion appliances (including incinerators) in the building.
Protection against pollution	
J6. Oil storage tanks and the pipes connecting them to combustion appliances shall- (a) be so constructed and protected as to reduce to a reasonable level the risk of the oil escaping and causing pollution; and (b) have affixed in a prominent position a durable notice containing information on how to respond to an oil escape so as to reduce to a reasonable level the risk of pollution.	Requirement J6 applies only to fixed oil storage tanks with capacities of 3500 litres or less, and connecting pipes, which are - (a) located outside the building; and (b) serve fixed combustion appliances (including incinerators) in a building used wholly or mainly as a private dwelling, but does not apply to buried systems.

Particular reference should be made to:

Approved Document B for guidance on compartmentation of buildings for fire safety purposes and for appropriate degrees of fire resistance for compartment boundaries.

Approved Document F for guidance on ventilation for health, and provision of extract ventilation using open flued combustion appliances.

Guidance on the UK implementation of European Standards for chimneys and flues

Guidance in this Approved Document draws on references to British Standards. In the life of this Approved Document, some of these British Standards will be withdrawn and be replaced by European standards for chimney and flue products.

The Department and a panel of the relevant British Standard committees has sponsored the publication of guidance on the application of the Construction Products Directive (CPD) to chimney products and information on how products specified by reference to European Standards (ENs) fits with the guidance in this Approved Document (see other publications referred to on Page 68).

Section 0

GENERAL GUIDANCE

Introduction to the provisions

0.1 This Approved Document gives guidance on how to satisfy the requirements of Part J. Although Part J applies to the accommodation of any combustion installation and liquid fuel storage system within the Limits on Application, the guidance in this Approved Document has been prepared mainly with domestic installations in mind, such as those comprising space and water heating systems and cookers and their flues, and their attendant oil and LPG fuel storage systems.

0.2 The guidance applies to combustion installations having power ratings and fuel storage capacities up to the limits shown in a) to c) below. Guidance which applies generally is given in this section and Section 1. More specific guidance is then given in:

a) Section 2 for solid fuel installations of up to 50kW rated output;

b) Section 3 for gas installations of up to 70kW net (77.7kW gross) rated input;

c) Section 4 for oil installations of up to 45kW rated heat output;

Section 5 gives guidance on requirement J5 for heating oil storage installations with capacities up to 3500 litres and liquefied petroleum gas (LPG) storage installations with capacities up to 1.1 tonne, although there is no size limit on the application of requirement J5. Section 5 also gives guidance on requirement J6, which is limited to installations where the capacity of the oil storage tank is 3500 litres or less, serving buildings used wholly or mainly as private dwellings.

0.3 For installations subject to the requirements of part J but outside the scope of this Approved Document, such as incinerators or installations with higher ratings than those mentioned above, specialist guidance may be necessary. However some larger installations may be shown to comply by adopting the relevant recommendations to be found in the *CIBSE Design Guide Volume B and practice standards produced by BSI and the Institution of Gas Engineers.*

Explanation of terms used

0.4 The following definitions have been adopted solely for the purposes of providing clarity in this Approved Document.

1. An **appliance compartment** is an enclosure specifically constructed or adapted to accommodate one or more gas or oil-fired appliances.

2. A **balanced compartment** is a method of installing an open-flued appliance into a compartment which is sealed from the remainder of the building and whose ventilation is so arranged in conjunction with the appliance flue as to achieve a balanced flue effect.

3. A **balanced flue** appliance is a type of room-sealed appliance which draws its combustion air from a point outside the building adjacent to the point at which the combustion products are discharged, the inlet and outlet being so disposed that wind effects are substantially balanced. Balanced flues may run vertically, but in the most common configuration they discharge horizontally through the external wall against which the appliance is situated.

4. The **boundary** is the boundary of the land or buildings belonging to and under the control of the building owner. Depending upon the paragraphs of this Approved Document to

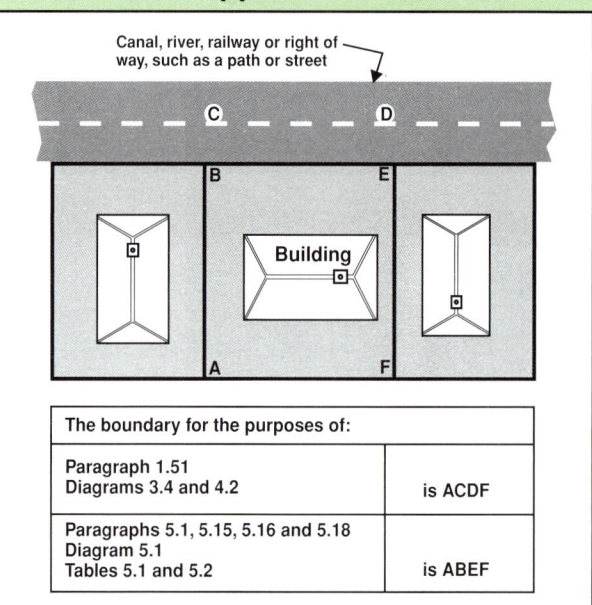

Diagram 0.1: **Boundaries in this Approved Document**

Canal, river, railway or right of way, such as a path or street

Building

The boundary for the purposes of:	
Paragraph 1.51 Diagrams 3.4 and 4.2	is ACDF
Paragraphs 5.1, 5.15, 5.16 and 5.18 Diagram 5.1 Tables 5.1 and 5.2	is ABEF

which it applies, it may be drawn only around the perimeter of the land in question or extended to the centreline of adjacent routes or waterways as shown in Diagram 0.1.

5. A **Building Control Body** is a body that carries out checks for compliance with the Building Regulations on plans of building work and on the building work itself. The Building Control Body may be either the Local Authority or an Approved Inspector. For further details, see the manual to the Building Regulations.

6. The **capacity** of an oil tank is its nominal volume as stated by the manufacturer. It is usually around 97% of the volume of liquid required to fill it to the brim.

7. A **chimney** is a structure consisting of a wall or walls enclosing one or more flues (see Diagram 0.2). In the gas industry, the chimney for a gas appliance is commonly called the flue.

8. A **combustion appliance** (or **appliance**) is an apparatus where fuel is burned to generate heat for space heating, water heating, cooking or other similar purpose. The appliance does not include systems to deliver fuel to it or for the distribution of heat. Typical combustion appliances are boilers, warm air heaters, water heaters, fires, stoves and cookers.

9. The **designation** system in BS EN 1443:1999 expresses the performance characteristics of a chimney or its components, as assessed in accordance with an appropriate European product standard, by means of a code such as EN1234 T400 P1 S W 1 R22 C50.

In the foregoing example, EN 1234 stands for the European standard in question and the remainder of the code gives classes of performance achieved in relation to that standard. For example, T400 indicates a product with a nominal working temperature of 400°C.

Chimney products tested in accordance with European standards may carry such a designation or a shorter Class to indicate which designation applies. For example, clay ceramic flue liners with the designation EN 1457 T600 N2 S D 3 are described as being of Class A1N2.

10. A **draught break** is an opening formed by a factory-made component into any part of the flue serving an open-flued appliance. Such openings may be provided to allow dilution air to be drawn into a flue or to lessen the effects of down-draught on combustion in the appliance.

Diagram 0.2: **Chimneys and flues**

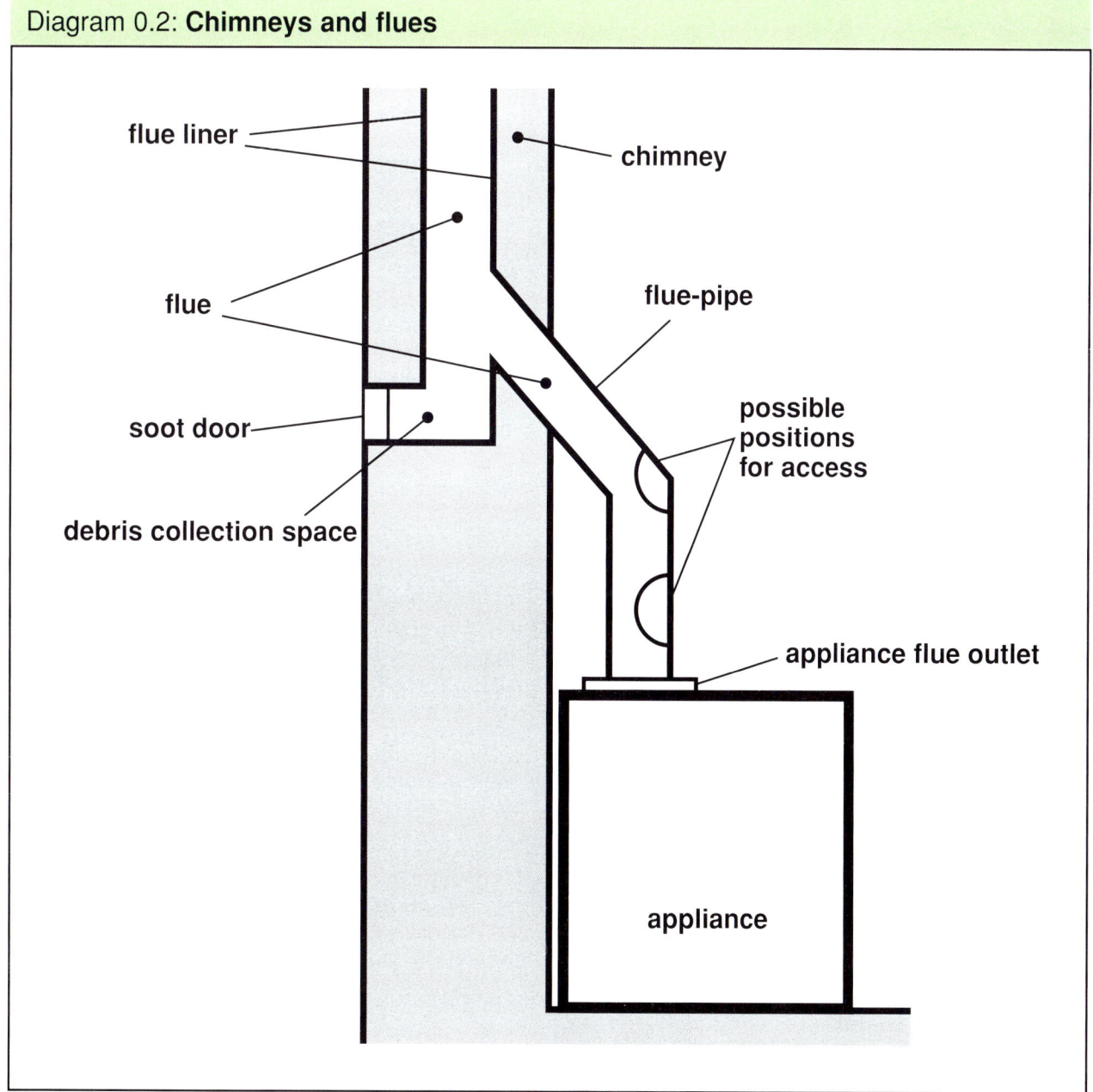

flue liner

chimney

flue

flue-pipe

soot door

possible positions for access

debris collection space

appliance flue outlet

appliance

Diagram 0.3: **Draught diverters and draught stabilisers**

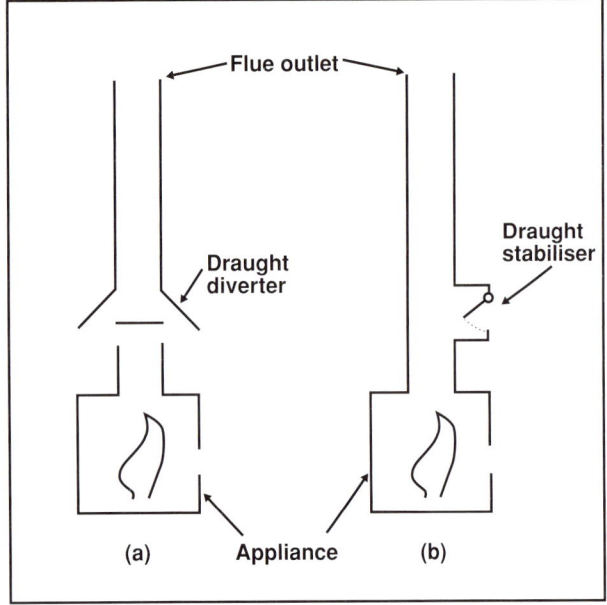

11.   A **draught diverter** is a form of draught break intended to prevent conditions in the main length of flue from interfering with the combustion performance of an open-flued appliance (see Diagram 0.3(a)). It allows the appliance to operate without interference from down-draughts that may occur in adverse wind conditions and excessive draught.

12.   A **draught stabiliser** is a factory made counter-balanced flap device admitting air to the flue, from the same space as the combustion air, to prevent excessive variations in the draught (see Diagram 0.3(b)). It is usual for these to be in the fluepipe or chimney, but they may be located on the appliance.

13.   **Factory-made metal chimneys** (also known as system chimneys) are prefabricated chimneys that are commonly manufactured as sets of components for assembly on site (although they can be supplied as one unit), having the performance appropriate for the intended appliance. They are available in various materials but typical types range from single walled metal chimneys suitable for some gas appliances to chimneys with insulation sandwiched between an inner liner and an outer metal wall which are designed for oil or solid fuel use.

14.   In a **fanned draught** installation, the proper discharge of the flue gases depends upon the operation of a fan, which may be separately installed in the flue or may be an integral part of the combustion appliance. Fans in combustion appliances may either extract flue gases from the combustion chamber or may cause the flue gases to be displaced from the combustion chamber if the fan is supplying it with air for combustion. Appliances with fans providing the combustion air (including most oil-fired and many gas-fired boilers) are also

commonly referred to as forced draught appliances (see Diagram 0.4). Flues in fanned draught installations run horizontally or vertically and can be at higher or lower pressures than their surroundings, dependent upon the location of the fan.

15.   A **fire compartment** is a building or part of a building comprising one or more rooms, spaces or storeys constructed to prevent the spread of fire to or from another part of the same building or an adjoining building. (A roof-space above the top storey of a fire compartment is included in that fire compartment). A **separated part** of a building is a form of compartmentation in which part of a building is separated from another part of the same building by a compartment wall. Such walls run the full height of the part and are in one vertical plane. Further information on this is given in Approved Document B (see Section 9 Compartmentation and Appendix C Methods of Measurement).

16.   A **fireplace recess** is a structural opening (sometimes called a builder's opening) formed in a wall or in a chimney breast, from which a chimney leads and which has a hearth at its base. Simple structural openings (Diagram 0.5(a)) are suitable for closed appliances such as stoves, cookers or boilers but gathers (Diagram 0.5(b)) are necessary for accommodating open fires. Fireplace recesses are often lined with firebacks to accommodate inset open fires (Diagram 0.5(c)). Lining components and decorative treatments fitted around openings reduce the opening area. It is the finished fireplace opening area which determines the size of flue required for an open fire in such a recess.

17.   **Fire resistance.** The fire resistance of a component or construction is a measure of its ability to withstand the effects of fire in one or more ways for a stated period of time. Guidance on determination of performance in terms of fire resistance is given in Approved Document B (Fire Safety).

18.   A **fire wall** is a means of shielding a fuel tank from the thermal radiation from a fire. For LPG tanks, it also ensures that gas accidentally leaking from the tank or fittings must travel by a longer path and therefore disperse safely, before reaching a hazard such as an opening in a building, a boundary or other potential ignition source.

19.   A **flue** is a passage that conveys the products of combustion from an appliance to the outside air (see Diagram 0.2).

20.   **Flueblock chimney** systems consist of a set of factory-made components, made from precast concrete, clay or other masonry units, that are designed for assembly on site to provide a complete chimney having the performance appropriate for the intended appliance. There are two types of common systems, one being solely for use with gas

burning appliances and the other, often called chimney block systems, being primarily designed for solid fuel burning appliances.

21.   A **flue box** is a factory made unit, usually made of metal, which is similar to a prefabricated appliance chamber except that it is designed to accommodate a gas burning appliance in conjunction with a factory-made chimney.

22   A **flueless appliance** is one which is designed to be used without connection to a flue. Its products of combustion mix with the surrounding room air and are eventually

transported to the outside as stale air leaves the room (see Diagram 0.4(g)).

23.   A **flue liner** is the wall of the chimney that is in contact with the products of combustion (see Diagram 0.2), such as a concrete flue liner, the inner liner of a factory-made chimney system or a flexible liner fitted into an existing chimney.

24.   A **flue outlet** is the point at which the products of combustion are discharged from the flue to the outside atmosphere, such as the top of a chimney pot or flue terminal.

Diagram 0.4: **Types of installation**

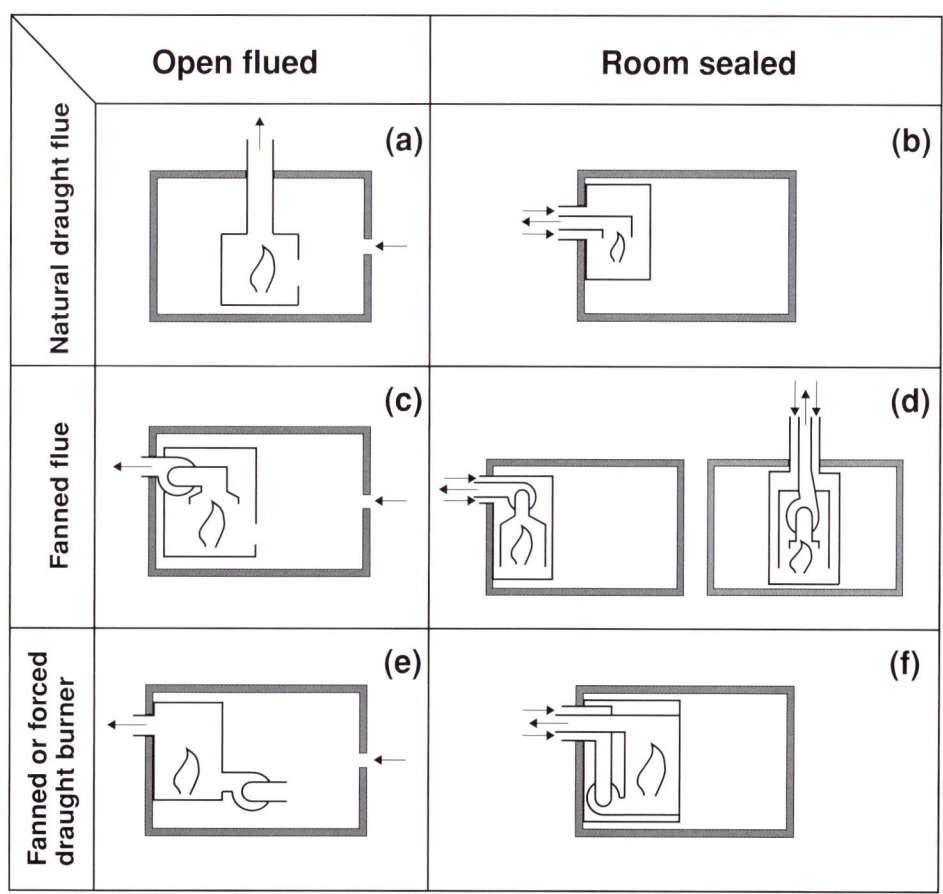

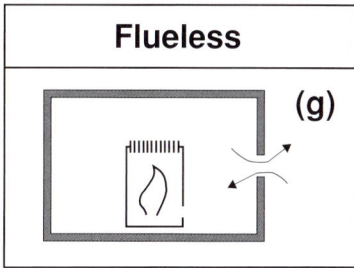

Note – For gas appliances only: CEN CR1749 classifies gas appliances according to their method of evacuating the products of combustion:

Type A – Flueless appliances

Type B – Open flued

Type C – Room sealed

The letters A, B and C are further qualified by numbers to identify the existence and mode of use of fans and draught diverters, as applicable. (e.g. B$_{11}$ for an open flued natural draught appliance with draught diverter)

Diagram 0.5: **Fireplace recesses**

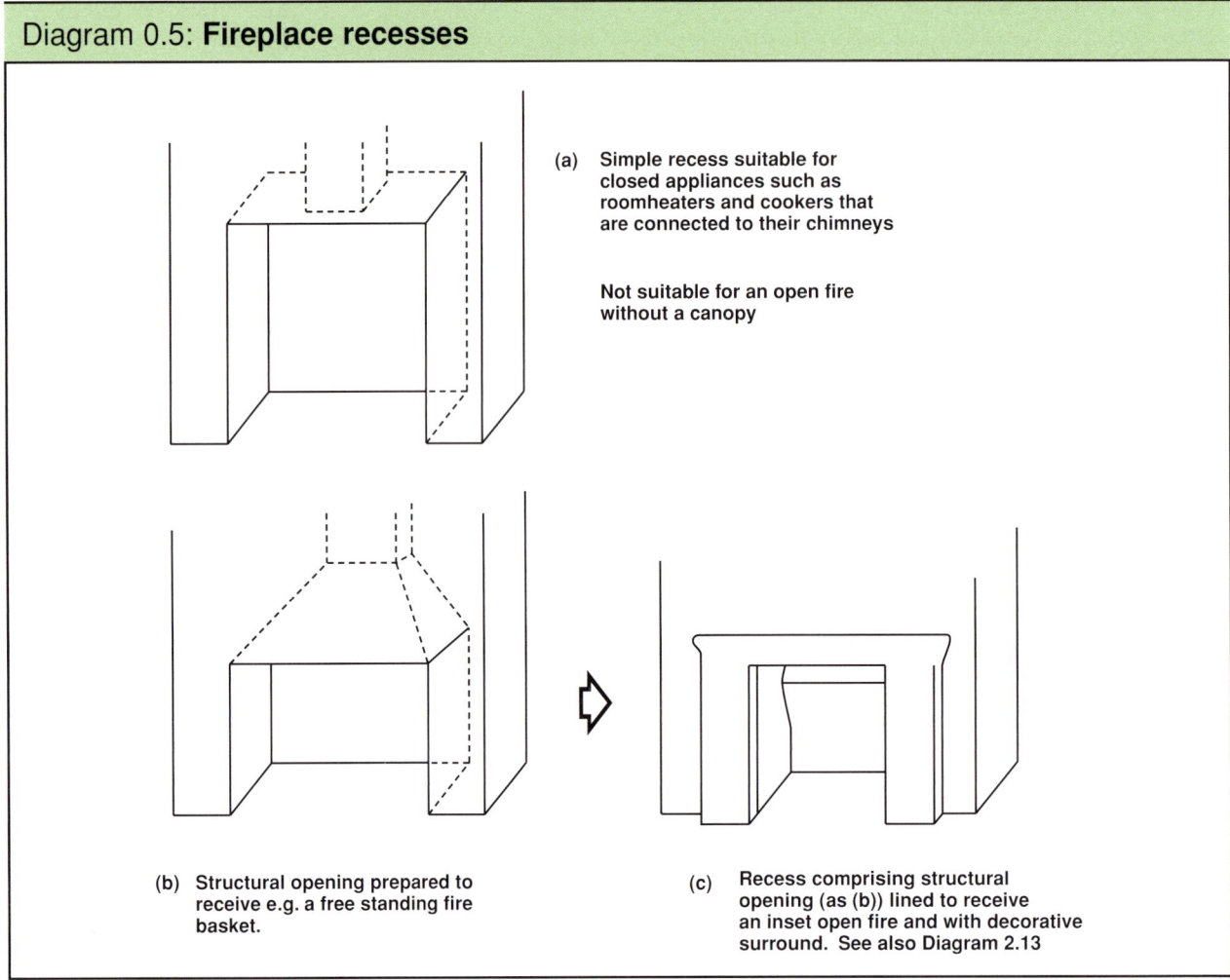

(a) Simple recess suitable for closed appliances such as roomheaters and cookers that are connected to their chimneys

Not suitable for an open fire without a canopy

(b) Structural opening prepared to receive e.g. a free standing fire basket.

(c) Recess comprising structural opening (as (b)) lined to receive an inset open fire and with decorative surround. See also Diagram 2.13

25.   A **fluepipe** is a pipe, either single walled (bare or insulated) or double walled, which connects a combustion appliance to a flue in a chimney. For clarity, when used in this way, it may be called a connecting fluepipe. (Fluepipe is also used to describe the tubular components from which some factory made chimneys for gas and oil appliances are made or from which plastic flue systems are made).

26.   A **hearth** is a base intended to safely isolate a combustion appliance from people, combustible parts of the building fabric and soft furnishings. The exposed surface of the hearth provides a region around the appliance which can be kept clear of anything at risk of fire. The body of the hearth may be thin insulating board, a substantial thickness of material such as concrete or some intermediate provision dependent upon the weight and downward heat emission characteristics of the appliance(s) upon it. For solid fuel open fires it is common to obtain the substantial thickness of material necessary by providing a constructional hearth, as part of the building structure, on which may be placed a decorative superimposed hearth to provide the clear surface (see Diagram 0.6).

27.   The **heat input rate** is the maximum rate of energy flow into a gas appliance that could be provided by the prevailing rate of fuel flow into the appliance, if the fuel were to be burned in an ideal manner, with full oxidation. It is calculated as the rate of fuel flow to the appliance multiplied by either the fuel's gross or net calorific value, depending upon whether or not it is assumed that conditions allow the latent heat due to the condensation of water in combustion products to be included in the heat obtained from the fuel. The gross calorific value includes the latent heat of condensation and the gross heat input rate is thus a larger figure than the net heat input rate. The calculation is entirely theoretical and either heat input rating could be used for any given appliance. However, it is now the norm to express the rating of a gas appliance as a net heat input rate (kW (net)).

28.   **Independently certified** products: see the explanation of "Independent certification schemes" in the Use of Guidance section on Page 3.

29.   **Installation instructions** are those instructions produced by manufacturers to enable installers to correctly install and test appliances and flues and to commission them into service.

30.   In a **natural draught** flue, the combustion products flow into the flue as a result of the buoyancy force produced due to the difference between the temperature of the gases within

Diagram 0.6: **The functions of hearths**

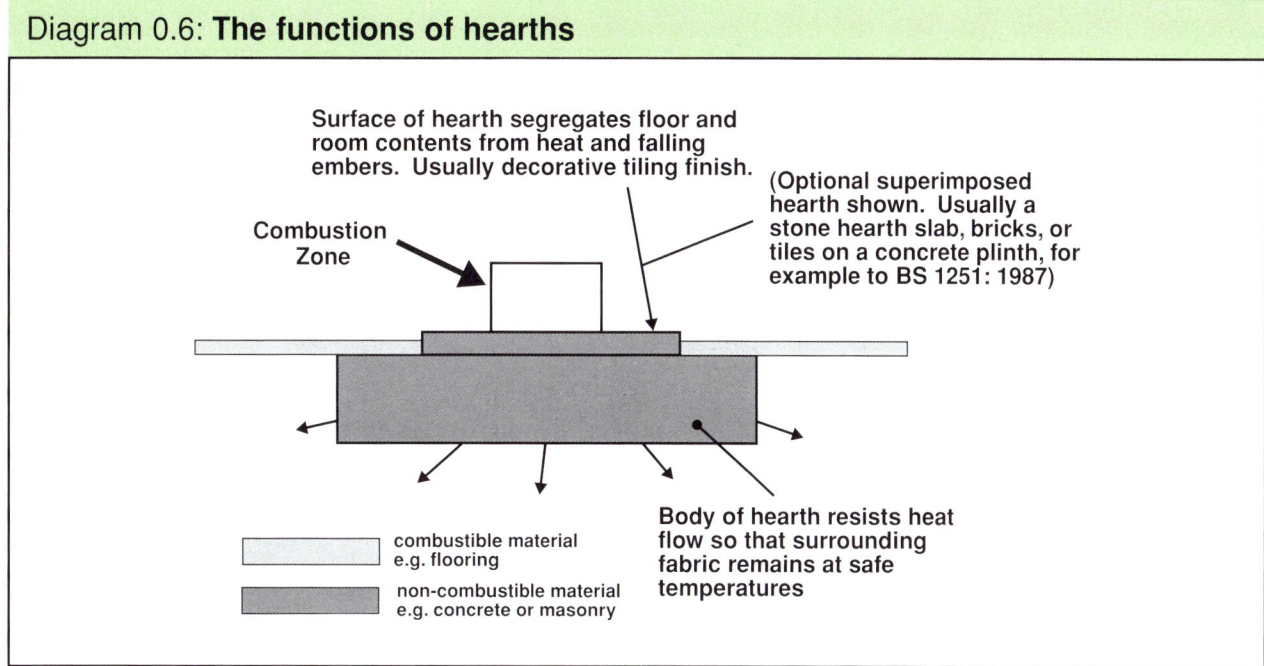

Surface of hearth segregates floor and room contents from heat and falling embers. Usually decorative tiling finish.

(Optional superimposed hearth shown. Usually a stone hearth slab, bricks, or tiles on a concrete plinth, for example to BS 1251: 1987)

Combustion Zone

combustible material e.g. flooring

non-combustible material e.g. concrete or masonry

Body of hearth resists heat flow so that surrounding fabric remains at safe temperatures

the flue and the temperature of the ambient air. Draught increases with the height of the flue. Except for those balanced flue appliances which are designed to discharge directly through the wall adjacent to the appliance, a satisfactory natural draught requires an essentially vertical run of flue (see Diagram 0.4 (a) and (b)).

31.   **Non-combustible material.** This is the highest level of reaction to fire performance. Non-combustible materials comprise:

a)   Any material which when tested to BS 476:11: 1982 (1988) does not flame nor cause any rise in temperature on either the centre (specimen) or furnace thermocouples; and

b)   Products classified as non-combustible in tests following the procedures in BS 476-4: 1970 (1984).

Typical examples of such materials to be found in buildings include totally inorganic materials such as concrete, fired clay, ceramics, metals, plaster and masonry containing not more than 1% by weight or volume of organic material. (Use in buildings of combustible metals such as magnesium-aluminium alloys should be assessed in each individual case).

32.   A **Notified Body**, for the purposes of the Gas Appliances (Safety) Regulations (1995), means:

a)   a body which is approved by the Secretary of State for Trade and Industry as being competent to carry out the required Attestation procedures for gas appliances and whose name and identification number has been notified by him/her to the Commission of the European Community and to other member States in accordance with the Gas Appliances (Safety) Regulations 1995;

b)   a body which has been similarly approved for the purposes of the Gas Appliances Directive by another member State and whose name and identification number has been notified to the Commission and to other member States pursuant to the Gas Appliances Directive.

33.   An **open-flued appliance** is one which draws its combustion air from the room or space within which it is installed and which requires a flue to discharge its products of combustion to the outside air (see Diagram 0.4 (a), (c) and (e)).

34.   A **prefabricated appliance chamber** is a set of factory-made pre-cast concrete components designed to provide a fireplace recess to accommodate an appliance such as a stove, and incorporates a gather when used with an open fire. The chamber is normally positioned against a wall and may be designed to support a chimney. The chamber and chimney are often enclosed to create a false chimney breast. (see also "flue box" defined in Paragraph 0.4 (21)).

35.   The **rated heat input** (sometimes shortened to rated input) for a gas appliance is the maximum heat input rate at which it can be operated, as declared on the appliance data plate. For gas appliances it is now the norm to express this rating as a net value (kW (net)) although the gross value (kW (gross)) was used until recently (see Paragraph 0.4 (27)).

36.   The **rated heat output** for an oil appliance is the maximum declared energy output rate (kW) as declared on the appliance data plate.

37.   The **rated heat output** for a solid fuel appliance is the maximum manufacturers' declared energy output rate (kW) for the appliance. This may be different for different fuels.

38.   A **room-sealed appliance** means an appliance whose combustion system is sealed from the room in which the appliance is located and which obtains air for combustion from a ventilated uninhabited space within the building or directly from the open air outside the building and which vents the products of combustion directly to open air outside the building (see Diagram 0.4 (b), (d) and (f)).

39.   A **throat** is a contracted part of the flue between a fireplace recess and its chimney (see Diagrams 2.6). Throats are usually formed from prefabricated components as shown in Diagram 2.13.

Measuring the size of flues and ducts

0.5   The size of a flue or duct (area, diameter etc) should be measured at right angles to the direction in which gases flow. Where offset components are used, they should not reduce the flue area to less than the minimum required for the combustion appliance (see Diagram 0.7).

Diagram 0.7: **Measurement of flues and ducts**

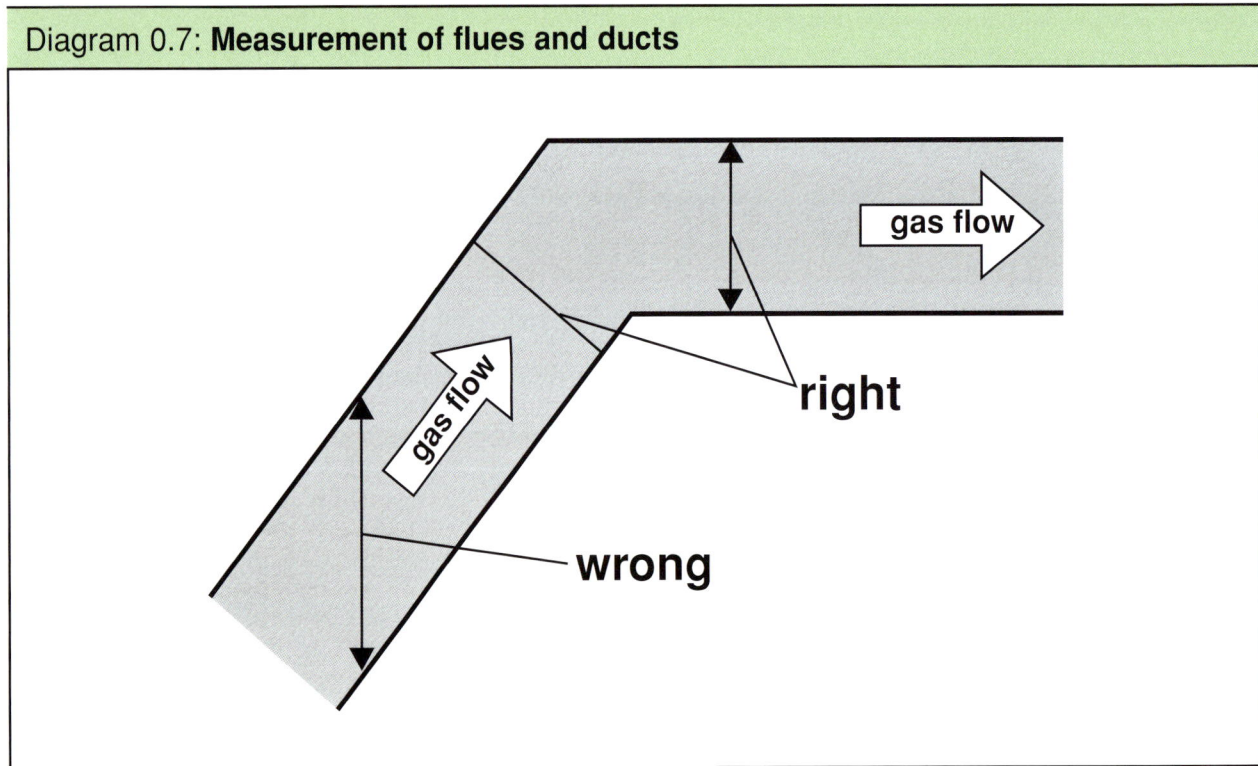

Section 1

PROVISIONS WHICH APPLY GENERALLY TO COMBUSTION INSTALLATIONS

Performance

1.1   In the Secretary of State's view requirements J1 to J4 will be met if the building provisions for the safe accommodation of combustion appliances:

a)   enable the admission of sufficient air for:

  i)   the proper combustion of fuel and the operation of flues; and

  ii)   the cooling of appliances where necessary;

b)   enable normal operation of appliances without the products of combustion becoming a hazard to health;

c)   enable normal operation of appliances without their causing danger through damage by heat or fire to the fabric of the building;

d)   have been inspected and tested to establish suitability for the purpose intended;

e)   have been labelled to indicate performance capabilities.

Air supply for combustion appliances

1.2   Combustion appliances require ventilation to supply them with air for combustion. Ventilation is also required to ensure the proper operation of flues or, in the case of flueless appliances, to ensure the products of combustion are safely dispersed to the outside air. In some cases, combustion appliances may also require air for cooling control systems and/or to ensure that casings remain safe to touch (see Diagram 1.1). General guidance on where it may be necessary to install air vents for these purposes is given below.

1.3   Air vent sizes, which are dependent upon the type of fuel burned, are given in Sections 2, 3 and 4 and are for one combustion appliance only. The air supply provisions will usually need to be increased where a room contains more than one appliance (such as a kitchen containing an open-flued boiler and an open-flued cooker).

Permanently open ventilation of rooms

1.4   A room containing an open-flued appliance may need permanently open air vents. An open-flued appliance must receive a certain amount of air from outside ("combustion air" in Diagram 1.1) dependent upon its type and rating. Infiltration through the building fabric may be sufficient but above certain appliance ratings permanent openings are necessary (see Diagram 1.1).

Permanent ventilation of appliance compartments

1.5   Appliance compartments that enclose open-flued combustion appliances should be provided with vents large enough to admit all of the air required by the appliance for combustion and proper flue operation, whether the compartment draws its air from a room or directly from outside (see Diagram 1.1(b and c)).

1.6   Where appliances require cooling air, appliance compartments should be large enough to enable air to circulate and high and low level vents should be provided (see Diagram 1.1(d, e, f and g)).

1.7   Where appliances are to be installed within balanced compartments (see Paragraph 0.4(2)), special provisions will be necessary and the appliance and ventilation system manufacturer's instructions should be followed.

Ventilation of other rooms or spaces

1.8   If an appliance is room-sealed but takes its combustion air from another space in the building (such as the roof void) or if a flue has a permanent opening to another space in the building (such as where it feeds a secondary flue in the roof void), that space should have ventilation openings directly to outside. Where the roof space is to be used as a source of air for a combustion installation serving a dwelling, the dwelling roof ventilation provisions suggested in Approved Document F would normally be satisfactory.

1.9   Where flued appliances are supplied with combustion air through air vents which open into adjoining rooms or spaces, the adjoining rooms or spaces should have air vent openings of at least the same size direct to the outside. Air vents for flueless appliances however, should open directly to the outside air.

Diagram 1.1: **General air supply to a combustion appliance**
(For sizes see Sections 2, 3 and 4)

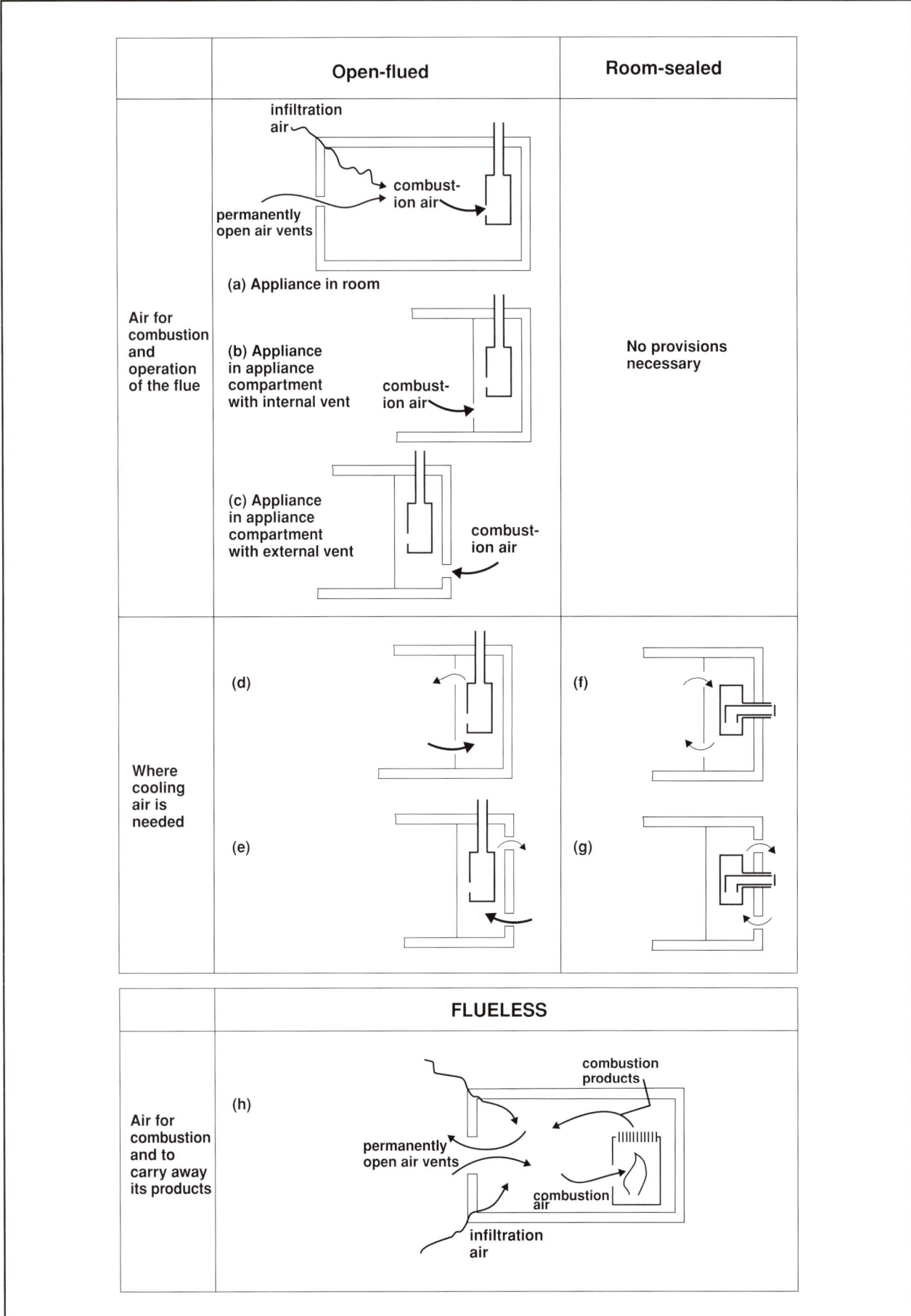

Diagram 1.2: **Ventilator free areas**

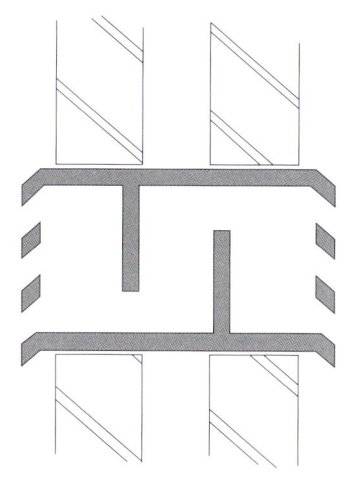

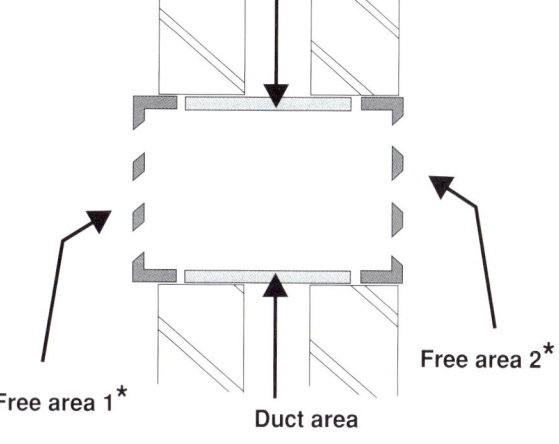

Free area 1*

Duct area

Free area 2*

(a) **Proprietary unit incorporating baffles, grilles etc: use the manufacturer's stated free area**

(b) **Ventilator assembled on site from components (* free area as marked on component or as measured by builder - see below)**
Use whichever is the smaller of Free area 1, Free area 2 or the Duct area

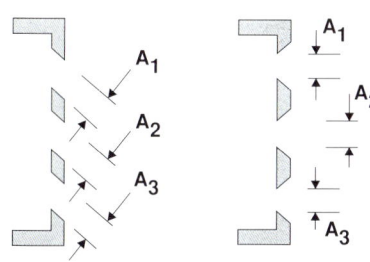

A_1

A_2

A_3

A_1

A_2

A_3

(c) **Measuring the free area of components on site**
Free area = A_1 + A_2 + A_3

Permanently open air vents

1.10 Permanently open air vents should be non-adjustable, sized to admit sufficient air for the purpose intended and positioned where they are unlikely to become blocked. Ventilators should be installed so that building occupants are not provoked into sealing them against draughts or noise. They should not be made in fire resisting walls other than external walls (although they should not penetrate those parts of external walls shielding LPG tanks). Air vents should not be located within a fireplace recess except on the basis of specialist advice.

1.11 A way of meeting the requirement would be to size permanently open air vents so that their free area or their equivalent free area if of a more complex design, is sufficient for the appliance(s) to be installed (taking account where necessary of obstructions such as grilles and anti vermin mesh), and to site them:

a)   outside fireplace recesses and beyond the hearths of open fires so that dust or ash will not be disturbed by draughts; and

b)   in a location unlikely to cause discomfort from cold draughts.

1.12 Where ventilation is to be provided via a single proprietary assembly, for example when it is proposed to use a proprietary ventilator with integral grilles to bridge a cavity wall, the equivalent free area of the ventilator may be taken to be the manufacturer's value (the manufacturer may call this a free area or equivalent free area) (see Diagram 1.2(a)).

1.13 Where two or more components are to be used to provide a non-proprietary assembly, the assembly should be kept as simple and smooth as possible. The assembly should be taken to have an equivalent free area equal to that of the component with the smallest free area in the assembly. The free area of each component should be its manufacturer's figure or, where that is not available, its free area measured in accordance with Paragraph 1.14 (see Diagram 1.2(b)).

1.14 The measured free area of a ventilator component is its total unobstructed cross sectional area, measured in the plane where this area is at a minimum and at right angles to the direction of air flow. For an airbrick, grille or louvre, it will be the aggregate free area of the individual apertures (see Diagram 1.2(c)).

1.15 Grilles or meshes protecting air vents from the entry of animals or birds should have aperture dimensions no smaller than 5 mm.

1.16 Discomfort from cold draughts can be avoided by placing vents close to appliances (for example by using floor vents), by drawing air from intermediate spaces such as hallways or by ensuring good mixing of incoming cold air by placing air vents close to ceilings. (see Diagrams 1.3, 1.4 and 1.5). In noisy areas, it may be necessary to install proprietary noise attenuated ventilators to limit the entry of noise into the building.

1.17 Buildings may have air tight membranes in their floors to isolate them from the ground below. Ventilation ducts or vents installed to supply air to combustion appliances should not penetrate these membranes in a way that will render them ineffective. Such membranes (including radon-proof membranes) are described in *BRE Report BR 414 (2001) and BRE Report BR 211 (1999)* which give guidance when service penetrations are necessary.

Provisions complying with both Part F and Part J.

1.18 Rooms or spaces intended to contain open-flued combustion appliances may need permanent ventilation to comply with Part J and adjustable ventilation to comply with Part F. Permanently open air vents for combustion appliances can be accepted in place of some or all of the adjustable background ventilation for health, dependent upon opening area and location. However adjustable vents installed to meet the requirements of Part F cannot be used as substitutes for the ventilation openings needed to comply with Part J unless they are fixed permanently open.

1.19 Rooms or spaces intended to contain flueless appliances may need: permanent ventilation and rapid ventilation (such as openable windows) to comply with Part J; and adjustable ventilation and rapid ventilation to comply with Part F. Permanent ventilation provisions to comply with Part J may be acceptable in place of adjustable ventilation provisions for Part F subject to the limitations described in Paragraph 1.18. Openable elements installed for the rapid ventilation of rooms and other provisions made for the rapid ventilation of kitchens, in order to comply with Part F, may be acceptable in place of openable elements for the rapid ventilation of rooms or spaces containing flueless appliances.

Diagram 1.3: **Location of permanent air vent openings, some examples**

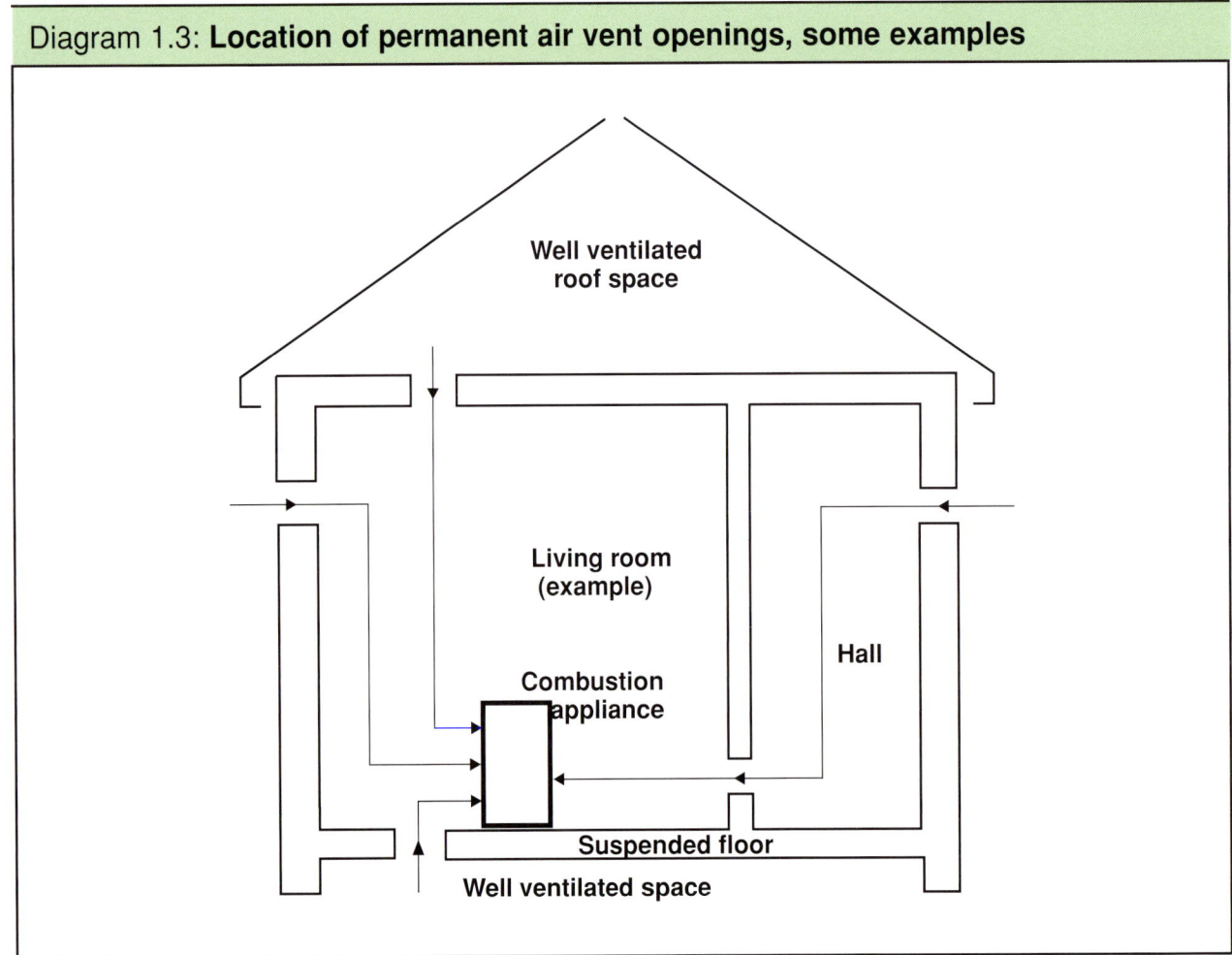

Well ventilated roof space

Living room (example)

Hall

Combustion appliance

Suspended floor

Well ventilated space

Diagram 1.4: **Provision of permanent air vent openings in a solid floor**

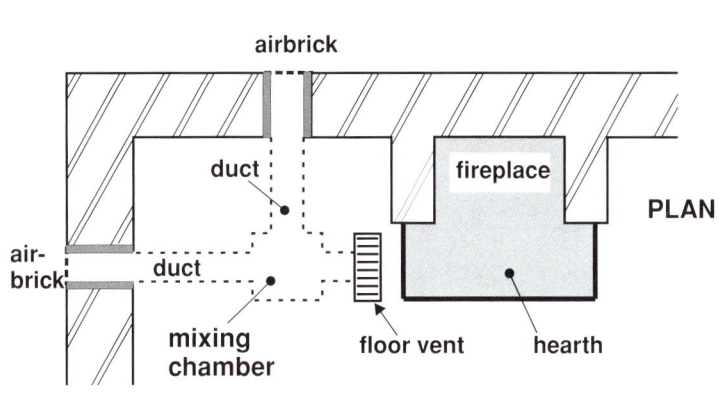

Airbrick, duct and grille should have an equivalent free area
at least that recommended in Sections 2,3 or 4 as relevant

Diagram 1.5: **Provision of ventilator communicating with a roof space (e.g. a loft)**

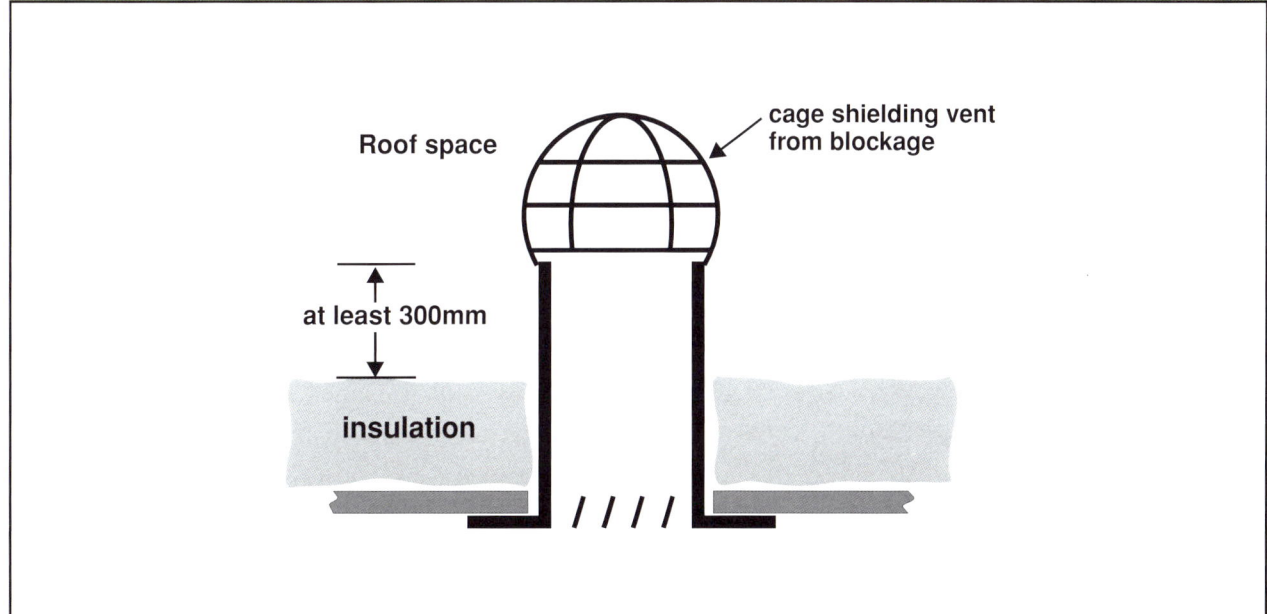

Interaction of mechanical extract ventilation and open-flued combustion appliances

1.20 Extract fans lower the pressure in a building, which can cause the spillage of combustion products from open flued appliances. This can occur even if the appliance and the fan are in different rooms. Ceiling fans produce air currents and hence local depressurisation which can also cause the spillage of flue gases from open-flued gas appliances or from solid fuel open fires. In buildings where it is intended to install open-flued combustion appliances and extract fans, the combustion appliances should be able to operate safely whether or not the fans are running. A way of showing compliance in these circumstances would be to follow the installation guidance below, and to show by tests that combustion appliances operate safely whether or not fans are running.

a) For gas appliances: where a kitchen contains an open-flued appliance, the extract rate of the kitchen extract fan should not exceed 20 litres/second (72m³/hour).

b) For oil appliances: limit fan capacities as described in *OFTEC Technical Information Note TI/112* and then carry out flue draught interference tests as described in *TI/112*.

c)　For solid fuel appliances: avoid installing extract ventilation in the same room or alternatively seek further guidance from HETAS (see Appendix F).

d)　For commercial and industrial installations, specialist advice may be necessary regarding the possible need for the interlocking of gas heaters and any mechanical ventilation systems.

e)　When fans are used to extract radon from below a building follow the guidance in *BRE Good Building Guide GBG 25*.

1.21 A suitable test would be to check for spillage when appliances are subjected to the greatest possible depressurisation. A prerequisite for this condition is that all external doors, windows and other adjustable ventilators to outside are closed. The depressurisation at the appliance will depend on the particular combination of fans in operation (fans in the room containing the appliance and fans elsewhere in the building) and the pattern of open internal doors, hatches etc which is established at the time of the test (when fans should be on their maximum useable setting), and the specific combination causing the greatest depressurisation at the appliance depends upon the circumstances in each case. Several tests (which should include a test with the door leading into the room of installation closed and all fans in that room switched on) may therefore be necessary to demonstrate the safe operation of the appliance with reasonable certainty. The effect of ceiling fans should be checked during the tests.

1.22 The presence of some fans may be obvious, such as those on view in kitchens, but others may be less obvious: fans installed in domestic appliances such as tumble dryers and fans fitted to other open flued combustion appliances can also contribute to depressurisation. In addition, fans may also be provided to draw radon gas from the ground below a building (see Paragraph 1.17).

1.23 The appliance manufacturer's installation instructions may describe a suitable spillage test for gas appliances but the procedure in BS 5440-1:2000 can be used. The effects of fans on oil-fired appliances can be checked by measuring the combustion conditions: the appliance should be shown to operate satisfactorily both with and without the fans running.

Provision of flues

1.24 Appliances other than flueless appliances should incorporate or be connected to suitable flues which discharge to the outside air.

1.25 This Approved Document provides guidance on how to meet the requirements in terms of constructing a flue or chimney, where each flue serves one appliance only. Flues designed to serve more than one appliance can meet the requirements by following the guidance in BS 5410-1:1997 for oil and BS 5440-1:2000 for gas-fired systems. However, each solid fuel appliance should have its own flue.

Condensates in flues

1.26 Chimneys and flues should provide satisfactory control of water condensation. Ways of providing satisfactory control include:

a)　for chimneys that do not serve condensing appliances, by insulating flues so that flue gases do not condense in normal operation;

b)　for chimneys that do serve condensing appliances:

　　i)　by using lining components that are impervious to condensates and suitably resistant to corrosion and by making appropriate provisions for draining, avoiding ledges, crevices etc;

　　ii)　making provisions for the disposal of condensate from condensing appliances.

Construction of masonry chimneys

1.27 New chimneys should be constructed with flue liners and masonry suitable for the intended application. Ways of meeting the requirement would be to use bricks, medium weight concrete blocks or stone (with wall thicknesses as given in Sections 2, 3 or 4 according to the intended fuel) with suitable mortar joints for the masonry and suitably supported and caulked liners. Liners suitable for solid fuel appliances (and generally suitable for other fuels) could be:

a)　liners whose performance is at least equal to that corresponding to the designation T450 N2 S D 3, as described in BS EN 1443:1999, such as:

　　i)　clay flue liners with rebates or sockets for jointing meeting the requirements for Class A1 N2 or Class A1 N1 as described in BS EN 1457:1999; or

　　ii)　concrete flue liners independently certified as meeting the requirements for the classification Type A1, Type A2, Type B1 or Type B2 as described in prEN 1857(e18) January 2001; or

　　iii)　other products that are independently certified as meeting the criteria in a).

b) imperforate clay pipes with sockets for jointing as described in BS 65: 1991 (1997).

1.28 Liners should be installed in accordance with their manufacturer's instructions. Appropriate components should be selected to form the flue without cutting and to keep joints to a minimum. Bends and offsets should only be formed with matching factory-made components. Liners need to be placed with the sockets or rebate ends uppermost to contain moisture and other condensates in the flue. Joints should be sealed with fire cement, refractory mortar or installed in accordance with their manufacturer's instructions. Spaces between the lining and the surrounding masonry should not be filled with ordinary mortar. In the absence of liner manufacturer's instructions, the space could be filled with a weak insulating concrete such as mixtures of:

a) one part ordinary Portland cement to 20 parts suitable lightweight expanded clay aggregate, minimally wetted; or

b) one part ordinary Portland cement to 6 parts Vermiculite; or

c) one part ordinary Portland cement to 10 parts Perlite.

Construction of flueblock chimneys

1.29 Flueblock chimneys should be constructed of factory-made components suitable for the intended application installed in accordance with manufacturer's instructions. Ways of meeting the requirement for solid fuel appliances (and generally suitable for other fuels) include using:

a) flueblocks whose performance is at least equal to that corresponding to the designation T450 N2 S D 3, as described in BS EN 1443:1999, such as:

  i) clay flueblocks at least meeting the requirements for Class FB1 N2 as described in BS EN 1806:2000;

  ii) other products that are independently certified as meeting the criteria in a);

b) blocks lined in accordance with Paragraph 1.27 and independently certified as suitable for the purpose.

1.30 Joints should be sealed in accordance with the flueblock manufacturer's instructions. Bends and offsets should only be formed with matching factory-made components.

Material change of use

1.31 Where a building is to be altered for different use (e.g. it is being converted into flats) the fire resistance of walls of existing masonry chimneys may need to be improved as shown in Diagram 1.6.

Diagram 1.6: **Material change of use: fire protection of chimneys passing through other dwellings**

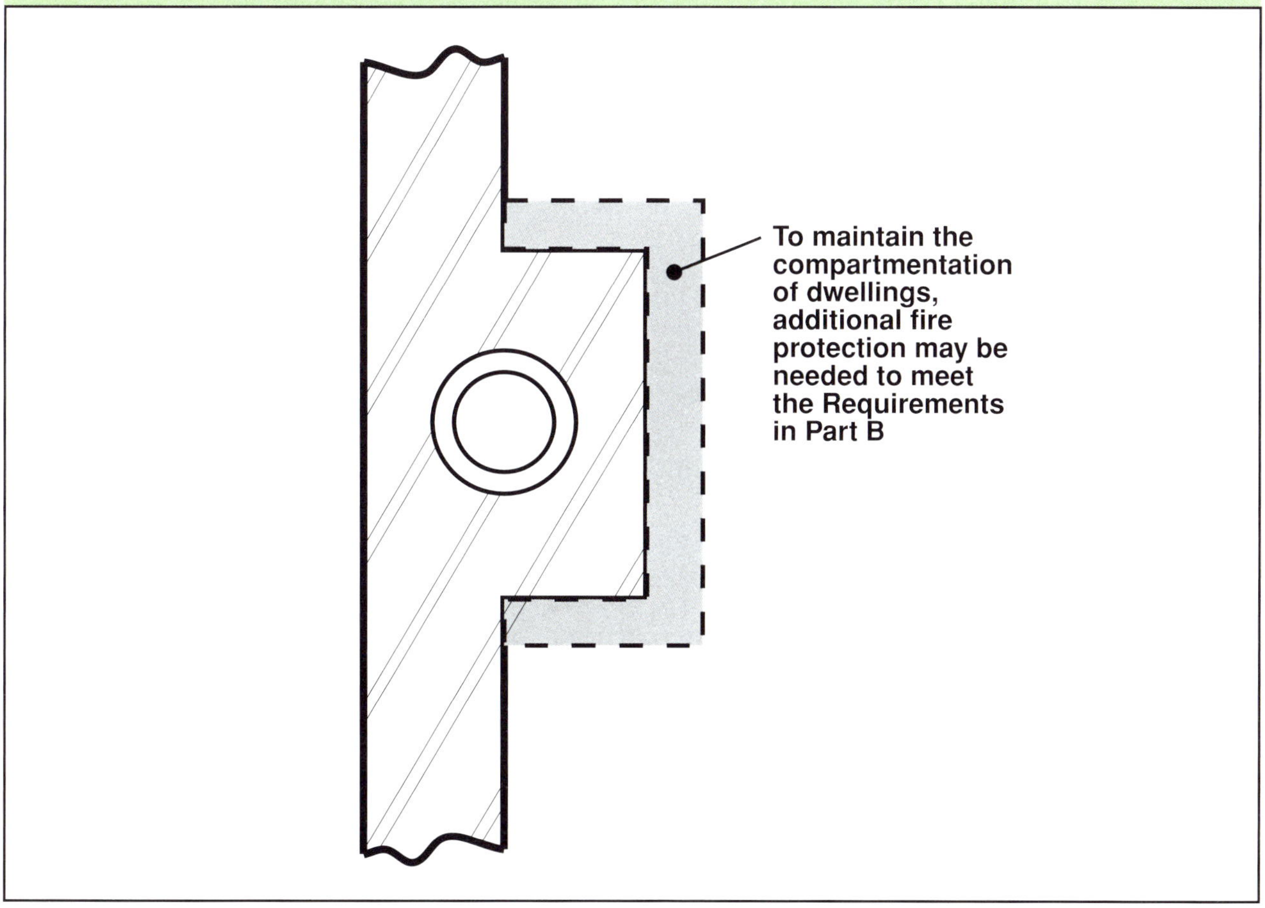

To maintain the compartmentation of dwellings, additional fire protection may be needed to meet the Requirements in Part B

Connecting fluepipes

1.32 Satisfactory components for constructing connecting fluepipes include:

a)   cast iron fluepipes complying with BS 41: 1973 (1998);

b)   mild steel fluepipes complying with BS 1449: Part 1: 1991, with a flue wall thickness of at least 3mm;

c)   pipes made from stainless steel as described in BS EN 10088-1: 1995 grades 1.4401, 1.4404, 1.4432 or 1.4436 with a flue wall thickness of at least 1mm;

d)   vitreous enamelled steel pipe complying with BS 6999: 1989 (1996);

e)   other fluepipes independently certified as having the necessary performance designation for suitable use with the intended appliance.

1.33 Fluepipes with spigot and socket joints should be fitted with the socket facing upwards to contain moisture and other condensates in the flue. Joints should be made gas-tight. A satisfactory way of achieving this would be to use proprietary jointing accessories or, where appropriate, by packing joints with non-combustible rope and fire cement.

Repair of flues

1.34 It is important to the health and safety of building occupants that renovations, refurbishments or repairs to flue liners should result in flues that comply with the requirements of J2 to J4. The test procedures referred to in paragraph 1.53 and in Appendix E can be used to check this.

1.35 Flues are controlled services as defined in Regulation 2 of the Building Reguations, that is to say they are services in relation to which Part J of Schedule 1 imposes requirements. If renovation, refurbishment or repair amounts to or involves the provision of a new or replacement flue liner, it is "building work" within the meaning of Regulation 3 of the Building Regulations. "Building work" and must not be undertaken without prior notification to the local authority. Examples of work that would need to be notified include:

(a)   relining work comprising the creation of new flue walls by the insertion of new linings such as rigid or flexible prefabricated components.

(b)   a cast in situ liner that significantly alters the flue's internal dimensions.

Anyone in doubt about whether or not any renovation, refurbishment or repair work involving a flue is notifiable "building work", could consult the building control department of their local authority, or an approved inspector.

Re-use of existing flues

1.36 Where it is proposed to bring a flue in an existing chimney back into use or to re-use a flue with a different type or rating of appliance, the flue and the chimney should be checked and, if necessary, altered to ensure that they satisfy the requirements for the proposed use. A way of checking before and/or after remedial work would be to test the flue using the procedures in Appendix E.

1.37 A way of refurbishing defective flues would be to line them using the materials and components described in Sections 2, 3, and 4 dependent upon the type of combustion appliance proposed. Before relining flues, they should be swept to remove deposits.

1.38 A flue may also need to be lined to reduce the flue area to suit the intended appliance. Oversize flues can be unsafe.

1.39 If a chimney has been relined in the past using a metal lining system and the appliance is being replaced, the metal liner should also be replaced unless the metal liner can be proven to be recently installed and can be seen to be in good condition.

Use of flexible metal flue liners for the relining of chimneys

1.40 A way of relining a chimney would be to use an independently certified flexible metal flue liner, specifically made to suit the types of fuels to be burnt. Flexible flue liners should only be used to reline a chimney and should not be used as the primary liner of a new chimney. They can be used to connect gas back boilers to chimneys where the appliance is located in a fireplace recess.

Use of plastic fluepipe systems

1.41 Plastic fluepipe systems can be acceptable in some cases, for example with condensing boiler installations, where the fluepipes are supplied by or specified by the appliance manufacturer, and approved by a Notified Body or independently certified as being suitable for purpose.

Factory-made metal chimneys

1.42 Ways of meeting the requirements when proposing factory-made metal chimneys include:

a)   using component systems independently certified as complying with the relevant sections of BS 4543-1:1990 (1996), BS 4543-2:1990 (1996) and BS 4543-3:1990 (1996) (Part 1 withdrawn April 2000; partially superseded by BS EN 1859:2000) and installing them in accordance with the relevant recommendations in BS 7566-1:1992 (1998), BS 7566-2:1992 (1998), BS 7566-3:1992 (1998) and BS 7566-4:1992 (1998);

Diagram 1.7: **The separation of combustible material from a factory made metal chimney meeting BS 4543: Part 1: 1990**

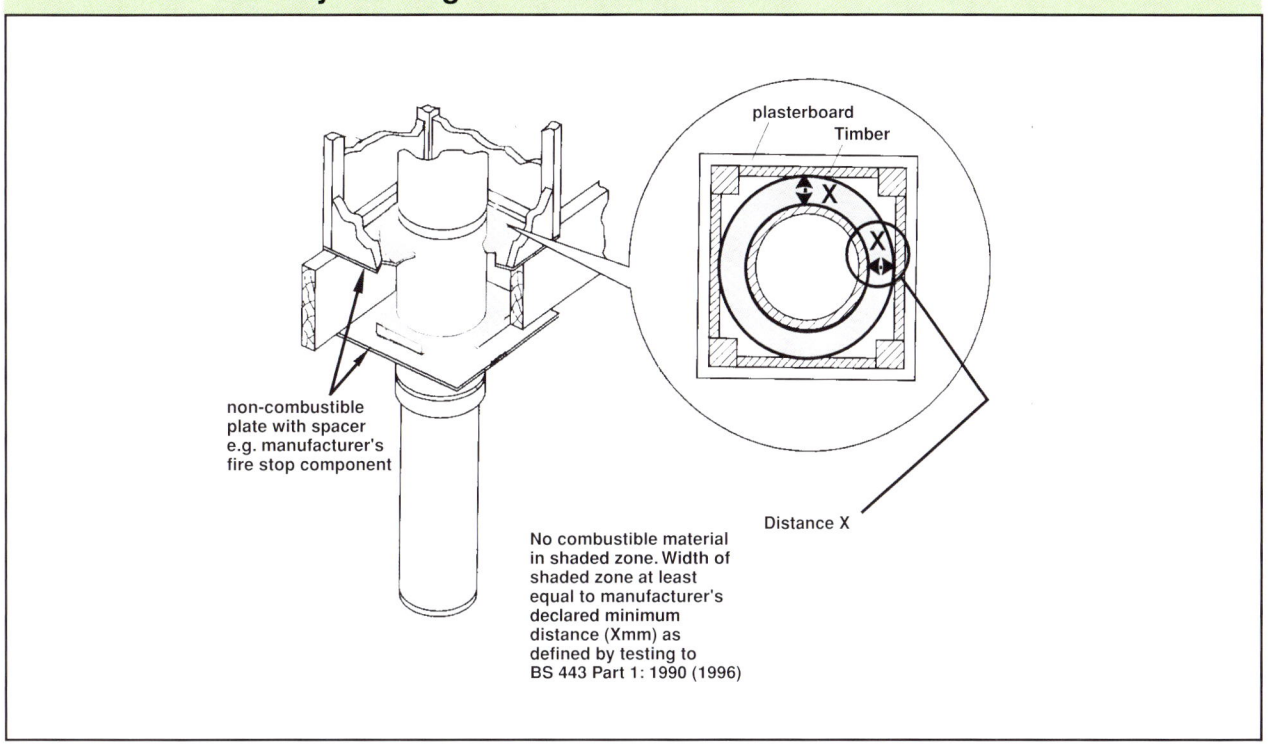

plasterboard
Timber

Distance X

non-combustible
plate with spacer
e.g. manufacturer's
fire stop component

No combustible material
in shaded zone. Width of
shaded zone at least
equal to manufacturer's
declared minimum
distance (Xmm) as
defined by testing to
BS 443 Part 1: 1990 (1996)

b)   for gas and for oil appliances where flue temperatures will not normally exceed 250°C, using twin wall component systems (and, for gas, single wall component systems) complying with BS 715:1993 and installing them in accordance with BS 5440-1:2000;

c) using any other chimney system that is independently certified as being suitable for the intended purpose and installed in accordance with the relevant recommendations in BS 7566-1:1992 (1998), BS 7566-2:1992 (1998), BS 7566-3:1992 (1998) and BS 7566-4:1992 (1998) or BS 5440-1:2000, as appropriate to the type of appliance being installed.

1.43 Where a factory-made metal chimney passes through a wall, sleeves should be provided to prevent damage to the flue or building through thermal expansion. To facilitate the checking of gas-tightness, joints between chimney sections should not be concealed within ceiling joist spaces or within the thicknesses of walls.

1.44 When providing a factory-made metal chimney, provision should be made to withdraw the appliance without the need to dismantle the chimney.

1.45 Factory-made metal chimneys should be kept a suitable distance away from combustible materials. Ways of meeting the requirement for chimneys complying with BS 4543-2:1990 (1996) or BS 4543-3:1990 (1996) comprise:

a)   locating the chimney not less than Distance "X" from combustible material, where

"X" is defined in BS 4543-1: 1990 (1996) as shown in Diagram 1.7;

b)   where a chimney passes through a cupboard, storage space or roof space, providing a guard placed no closer to the outer wall of the chimney than the distance in a) above.

1.46 Where a factory made metal chimney penetrates a fire compartment wall or floor, it must not breach the fire separation requirements of Part B. See Approved Document B for more guidance but the requirements may be met by:

a)   using a factory-made metal chimney of the appropriate level of fire resistance; or

b)   casing the chimney in non combustible material giving at least half the fire resistance recommended for the fire compartment wall or floor.

Configuration of natural draught flues serving open-flued appliances

1.47 Flue systems should offer least resistance to the passage of flue gases by minimising changes in direction or horizontal length. A way of meeting the requirement would be to build flues so that they are straight and vertical except for the connections to combustion appliances with rear outlets where the horizontal section should not exceed 150mm. Where bends are essential, they should be angled at no more than 45° to the vertical.

Diagram 1.8: **Bends in flues**

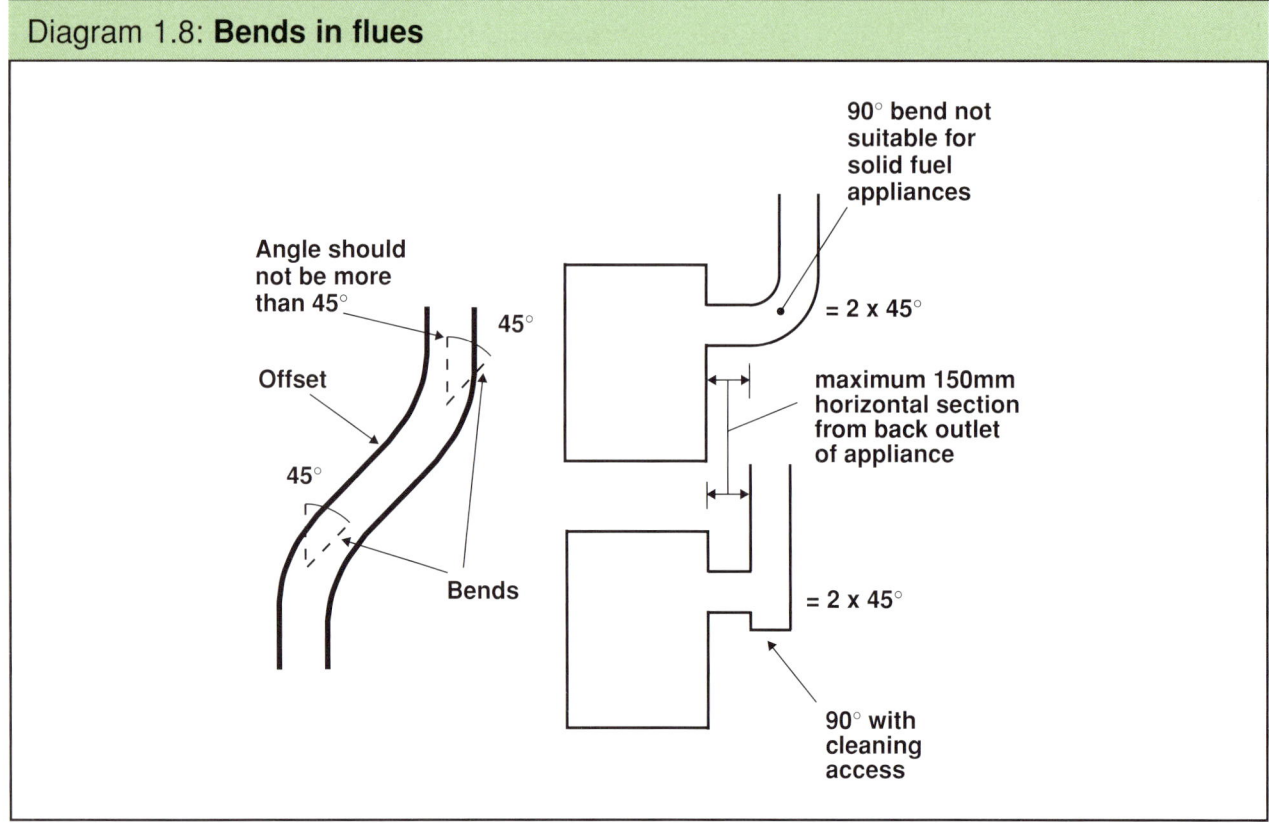

1.48 Provisions should be made to enable flues to be swept and inspected. A way of making reasonable provision would be to limit the number of changes of direction between the combustion appliance outlet and the flue outlet to not more than four 45° bends with not more than two of these being between an intended point of access for sweeping and either another point of access for sweeping or the flue outlet. (90° factory made bends, elbows or Tee pieces in fluepipes may be treated as being equal to two 45° bends (see Diagram 1.8)).

Inspection and cleaning openings in flues

1.49 A flue should not have openings into more than one room or space except for the purposes of:

a)   inspection or cleaning; or

b)   fitting an explosion door, draught break, draught stabiliser or draught diverter.

1.50 Openings for inspection and cleaning should be formed using purpose factory-made components compatible with the flue system, having an access cover that has the same level of gas-tightness as the flue system and an equal level of thermal insulation. Openings for cleaning the flue should allow easy passage of the sweeping brush. Covers should also be non-combustible except where fitted to combustible fluepipe (such as plastic fluepipe). After the appliance has been installed, it should be possible to sweep the whole flue.

Flues discharging at low level near boundaries

1.51 Flues discharging at low level near boundaries should do so at positions where the building owner will always be able to ensure safe flue gas dispersal. A way of achieving this where owners of adjacent land could build up to the boundary would be to adopt the suggestions in Diagrams 3.4 or 4.2, as relevant.

Dry lining around fireplace openings

1.52 Where a decorative treatment, such as a fireplace surround, masonry cladding or dry lining is provided around a fireplace opening, any gaps that could allow flue gases to escape from the fireplace opening into the void behind the decorative treatment, should be sealed to prevent such leakage. The sealing material should be capable of remaining in place despite any relative movement between the decorative treatment and the fireplace recess.

Condition of combustion installations at completion

1.53 Responsibility for achieving compliance with the requirements of Part J rests with the person carrying out the work. That "person" may be, e.g., a specialist firm directly engaged by a private client or it may be a developer or main contractor who has carried out work subject to Part J or engaged a sub-contractor to carry it out. In order to document the steps taken to achieve compliance with the requirements, a report should be drawn up showing that materials and components appropriate to the intended application have been used and that flues have passed appropriate tests. A suggested checklist for such a report is given at Appendix A and guidance on testing is given at Appendix E. Other forms of report may be acceptable. Specialist firms should provide the report to the client, developer or main contractor, who may be asked for documentation by the building control body.

1.54 Flues should be checked at completion to show that they are free from obstructions, satisfactorily gas-tight and constructed with materials and components of sizes which suit the intended application. Where the building work includes the installation of a combustion appliance, tests should cover fluepipes and [the gas-tightness of] joints between fluepipes and combustion appliance outlets. A spillage test to check for compliance with J2 should be carried out with the appliance under fire, as part of the process of commissioning to check for compliance with Part L, and (in relevant cases) as required by the Gas Safety (Installation and Use) Regulations.

1.55 Hearths should be constructed with materials and components of sizes to suit the intended application and should show the area where combustible materials should not intrude.

Notice plates for hearths and flues (Requirement J4)

1.56 Where a hearth, fireplace (including a flue box), flue or chimney is provided or extended (including cases where a flue is provided as part of the refurbishment work), information essential to the correct application and use of these facilities should be permanently posted in the building. A way of meeting this requirement would be to provide a notice plate as shown in Diagram 1.9 conveying the following information:

a)   the location of the hearth, fireplace (or flue box) or the location of the beginning of the flue;

b)   the category of the flue and generic types of appliances that can be safely accommodated;

c)   the type and size of the flue (or its liner if it has been relined) and the manufacturer's name;

d)   the installation date.

1.57 Notice plates should be robust, indelibly marked and securely fixed in an unobtrusive but obvious position within the building such as:

a)   next to the electricity consumer unit; or

b)   next to the chimney or hearth described; or

c)   next to the water supply stop-cock.

1.58 For chimney products whose performance characteristics have been assessed in accordance with a European Standard (EN) and which are supplied or marked with a designation as described in Paragraph 0.4 (9), the installer may optionally include this designation on the label as shown in Diagram 1.9.

Access to combustion appliances for maintenance

1.59 There should be a permanent means of safe access to appliances for maintenance. For appliances installed in roof spaces, walkways may be necessary for this purpose.

Diagram 1.9: **Example notice plate for hearths and flues**

Essential information	**IMPORTANT SAFETY INFORMATION** **This label must not be removed or covered**
	Property address .... *20 Main Street* *New Town*
	The hearth and chimney installed in the .... *lounge* are suitable for .... *decorative fuel effect gas fire* Chimney liner .... *double skin stainless steel flexible, 200mm diameter* Suitable for condensing appliance .... *no* Installed on .... *date*
Optional additional information	Other information (optional) .... *Designation of stainless steel liner stated by manufacturer to be T450 N2 S D 3* *e.g. installer's name, product trade names, installation and maintenance advice, European chimney product designations, warnings on performance limitations of imitation elements e.g. false hearths.*

Section 2

ADDITIONAL PROVISIONS FOR APPLIANCES BURNING SOLID FUEL WITH A RATED OUTPUT UP TO 50KW

Note: This section should be read in conjunction with Sections 0 and 1

Air supply to appliances

2.1 A way of meeting the requirement would be to adopt the general guidance given in Section 1, beginning at Paragraph 1.2, in conjunction with the guidance below.

2.2 Any room or space containing an appliance should have a permanent air vent opening of at least the size shown in Table 2.1. For appliances designed to burn a range of different solid fuels the air supply should be designed to accommodate burning the fuel that produces the highest heating output.

2.3 Some manufacturers may specify even larger areas of permanently open air vents or omit to specify a rated output (for example in the case of a cooker). In these cases, manufacturers installation instructions should be followed.

Size of flues

2.4 Fluepipes should have the same diameter or equivalent cross sectional area as that of the appliance flue outlet and should not be smaller than the size recommended by the appliance manufacturer.

2.5 Flues should be at least the size shown in Table 2.2 relevant to the particular appliance, and not less than the size of the appliance flue outlet or that recommended by the appliance manufacturer.

2.6 For multifuel appliances, the flue should be sized to accommodate burning the fuel that requires the largest flue.

2.7 For fireplaces with openings larger than 500mm x 550mm or fireplaces exposed on two or more sides (such as a fireplace under a canopy or open on both sides of a central chimney breast) a way of showing compliance would be to provide a flue with a cross sectional area equal to 15% of the total face area of the fireplace opening(s) (see Appendix B). However, specialist advice should be sought when proposing to construct flues having an area of:

a) more than 15% of the total face area of the fireplace openings; or

b) more than 120,000mm^2 (0.12m^2).

Table 2.1: **Air supply to solid fuel appliances**

Type of appliance	Type and amount of ventilation (1)	
Open appliance, such as an open fire with no throat, e.g. a fire under a canopy as in Diagram 2.7.	Permanently open air vent(s) with a total free area of at least 50% of the cross sectional area of the flue.	
Open appliance, such as an open fire with a throat as in Diagrams 2.6 and 2.13.	Permanently open air vent(s) with a total free area of at least 50% of the throat opening area. (2)	
Other appliance, such as a stove, cooker or boiler, with a flue draught stabiliser.	Permanently open air vent(s) as below:(3)	
		Total free area
	First 5kW of appliance rated output	300mm^2/kW
	Balance of rated output	850mm^2/kW
Other appliance, such as a stove, cooker or boiler, with no flue draught stabiliser.	A permanent air entry opening or openings with a total free area of at least 550mm^2 per kW of appliance rated output above 5kW.	

Notes:

1. Divide the area given in mm^2 by 100 to find the corresponding area in cm^2

2. For simple open fires as depicted in Diagram 2.13, the requirement can be met with room ventilation areas as follows:

Nominal fire size (fireplace opening size)	500mm	450mm	400mm	350mm
Total free area of permanently open air vents	20,500mm^2	18,500mm^2	16,500mm^2	14,500mm^2

3. Example: an appliance with a flue draught stabiliser and a rated output of 7kW would require a free area of: [5 x 300] + [2 x 850] = 3200mm^2

Table 2.2: **Size of flues in chimneys**

Installation (1)	Minimum flue size
Fireplace with an opening of up to 500mm x 550mm.	200mm diameter or rectangular/square flues having the same cross sectional area and a minimum dimension not less than 175mm.
Fireplace with an opening in excess of 500mm x 550mm or a fireplace exposed on two or more sides.	See Paragraph 2.7. If rectangular/square flues are used the minimum dimension should not be less than 200mm.
Closed appliance of up to 20kW rated output which: a) burns smokeless or low volatiles fuel(2); or b) is an appliance which meets the requirements of the Clean Air Act when burning an appropriate bituminous coal (3).	125mm diameter or rectangular/square flues having the same cross sectional area and a minimum dimension not less than 100mm for straight flues or 125mm for flues with bends or offsets.
Other closed appliance of up to 30kW rated output burning any fuel.	150mm diameter or rectangular/square flues having the same cross sectional area and a minimum dimension not less than 125mm.
Closed appliance of above 30kW and up to 50kW rated output burning any fuel.	175mm diameter or rectangular/square flues having the same cross sectional area and a minimum dimension not less than 150mm.

Notes:

1. Closed appliances include cookers, stoves, room heaters and boilers.

2. Fuels such as bituminous coal, untreated wood or compressed paper are not smokeless or low volatiles fuels.

3. These appliances are known as "exempted fireplaces".

Height of flues

2.8   Flues should be high enough to ensure sufficient draught to clear the products of combustion. The height necessary for this will depend upon the type of the appliance, the height of the building, the type of flue and the number of bends in it, and a careful assessment of local wind patterns. However, a flue height of 4.5m could be satisfactory if the guidance in Paragraphs 2.10 to 2.12 is adopted. As an alternative approach, the calculation procedure within BS 5854:1980 (1996) can be used as the basis for deciding whether a chimney design will provide sufficient draught.

2.9   The height of a flue serving an open fire is measured vertically from the highest point at which air can enter the fireplace to the level at which the flue discharges into the outside air. The highest point of air entry into the fireplace could be the top of the fireplace opening or, for a fire under a canopy, the bottom of the canopy.

Outlets from flues

2.10   The outlet from a flue should be above the roof of the building in a position where the products of combustion can discharge freely and will not present a fire hazard, whatever the wind conditions.

2.11   Flue outlet positions which can meet the requirements in common circumstances are shown in Diagram 2.1. The chimney heights and/or separations shown may need to be increased in particular cases where wind exposure, surrounding tall buildings, high trees or high ground could have adverse effects on flue draught.

2.12   A way of meeting the requirements where flues discharge on or in close proximity to roofs with surfaces which are readily ignitable, such as where roofs are covered in thatch or shingles, would be to increase the clearances to flue outlets to those shown in Diagram 2.2.

Connecting fluepipes

2.13   For connecting fluepipes a way of meeting the requirements would be to follow the general guidance in Paragraphs 1.32 and 1.33.

Location and shielding of connecting fluepipes

2.14   Connecting fluepipes should only be used to connect appliances to their chimneys. They should not pass through any roof space, partition, internal wall or floor, except to pass directly into a chimney through either a wall of the chimney or a floor supporting the chimney. Connecting fluepipes should also be guarded if they could be at risk of damage or if the burn hazard they present to people is not immediately apparent.

2.15   Connecting fluepipes should be located so as to avoid igniting combustible material. Ways of meeting the requirement include minimising horizontal and sloping runs and:

a)   separation by not less than three-quarters of the outside diameter of ordinary insulated pipes if the insulation is at least 12mm thick and has thermal conductivity not exceeding 0.065W/mK; or

b)   separation by shielding in accordance with Diagram 2.3; or

c)   following the guidance in Paragraph 1.45 where the connecting fluepipe is a factory-made metal chimney.

Diagram 2.1: **Flue outlet positions for solid fuel appliances**

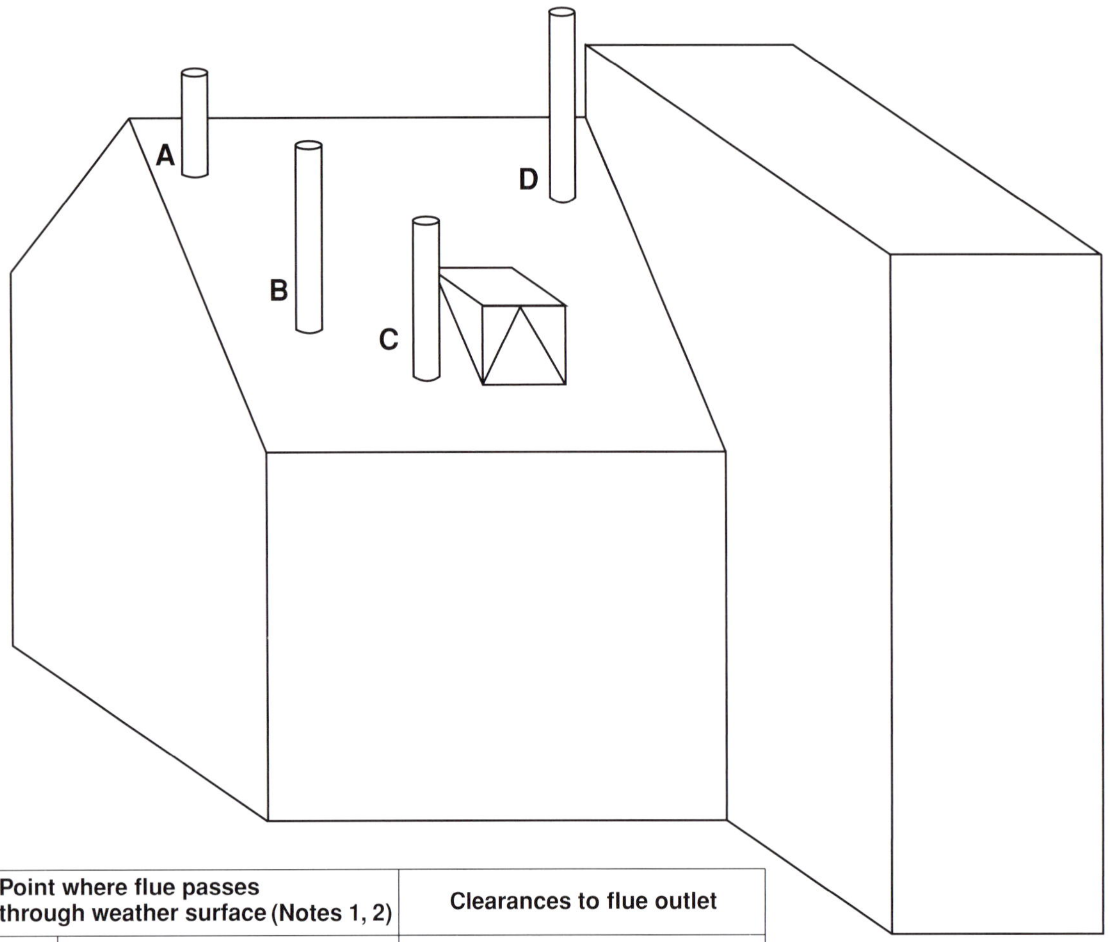

Point where flue passes through weather surface (Notes 1, 2)		Clearances to flue outlet
A	at or within 600mm of the ridge.	at least 600mm above the ridge.
B	elsewhere on a roof (whether pitched or flat)	at least 2300mm horizontally from the nearest point on the weather surface and: a) at least 1000mm above the highest point of intersection of the chimney and the weather surface; or b) at least as high as the ridge.
C	below (on a pitched roof) or within 2300mm horizontally to an openable rooflight, dormer window or other opening. (Note 3)	at least 1000mm above the top of the opening.
D	within 2300mm of an adjoining or adjacent building, whether or not beyond the boundary. (Note 3)	at least 600mm above the adjacent building.

Notes
1) The weather surface is the building external surface, such as its roof, tiles or external walls
2) A flat roof has a pitch less than 10°
3) The clearances given for A or B, as appropriate, will also apply.

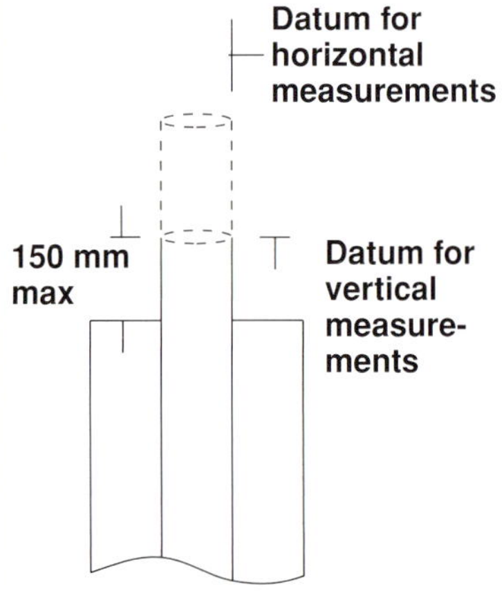

Datum for horizontal measurements

150 mm max

Datum for vertical measure-ments

The datum for vertical measurements is the point of discharge of the flue, or 150 mm above the insulation, whichever is the lower

Diagram 2.2 : **Flue outlet positions for solid fuel appliances – clearances to easily ignited roof coverings**
(Note: This diagram needs to be read in conjunction with Diagram 2.1)

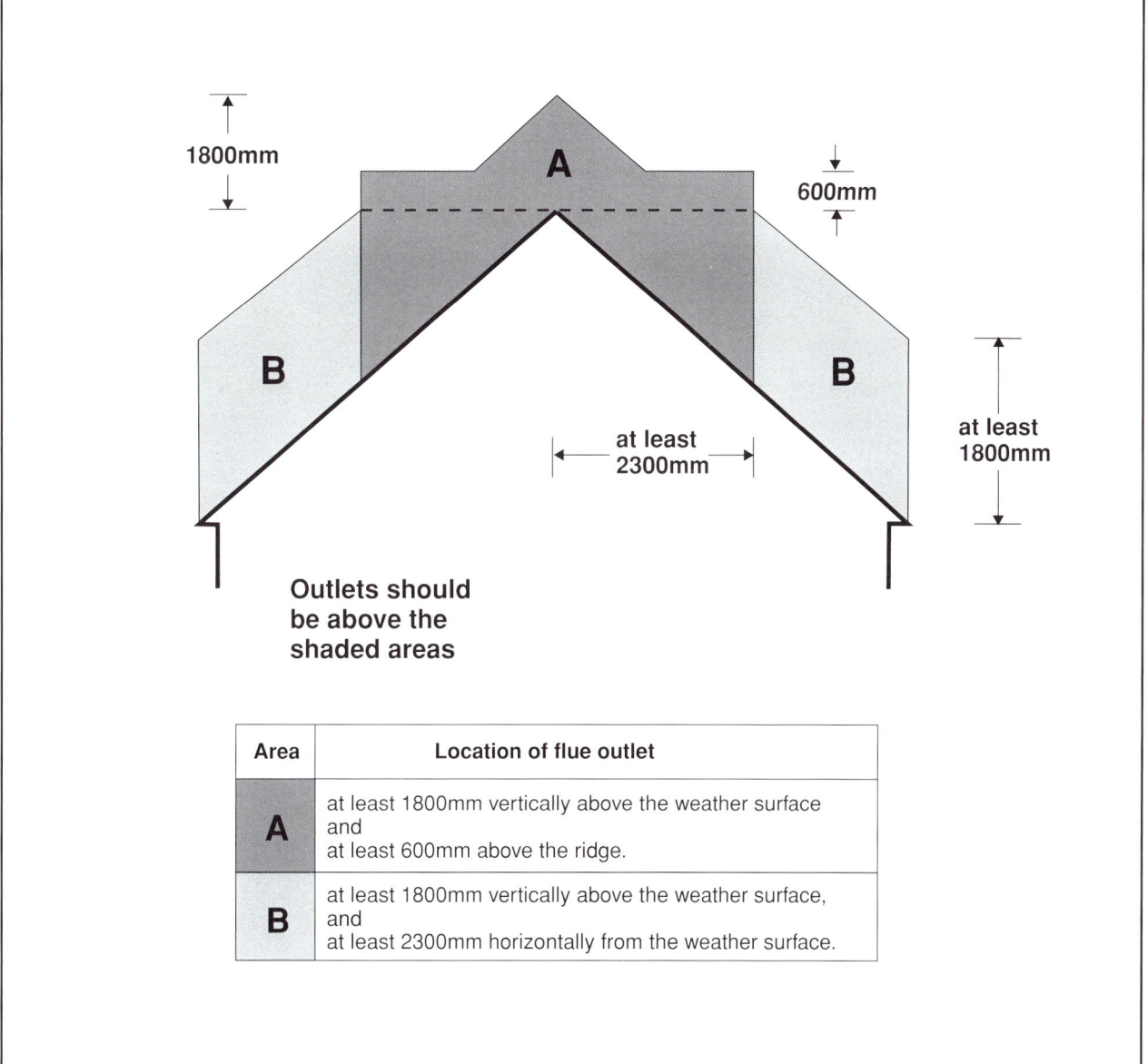

Area	Location of flue outlet
A	at least 1800mm vertically above the weather surface and at least 600mm above the ridge.
B	at least 1800mm vertically above the weather surface, and at least 2300mm horizontally from the weather surface.

Debris collection space

2.16 Where a chimney cannot be cleaned through the appliance, a debris collecting space which is accessible for emptying, and suitably sized opening(s) for cleaning should be provided at appropriate locations in the chimney.

Masonry and flueblock chimneys

2.17 Masonry chimneys should be built in accordance with Paragraphs 1.27 and 1.28. Flueblock chimneys should be built in accordance with Paragraphs 1.29 and 1.30. The thickness of the walls around the flues, excluding the thickness of any flue liners, should be in accordance with Diagram 2.4.

Separation of combustible material from fireplaces and flues

2.18 Combustible material should not be located where it could be ignited by the heat dissipating through the walls of fireplaces or flues. A way of meeting the requirement would be to follow the guidance in Diagram 2.5 so that combustible material is at least:

a) 200mm from the inside surface of a flue or fireplace recess; or

b) 40mm from the outer surface of a masonry chimney or fireplace recess unless it is a floorboard, skirting board, dado or picture rail, mantel-shelf or architrave. Metal fixings in contact with combustible materials should be at least 50mm from the inside surface of a flue.

Diagram 2.3: Protecting combustible material from uninsulated fluepipes for solid fuel appliances

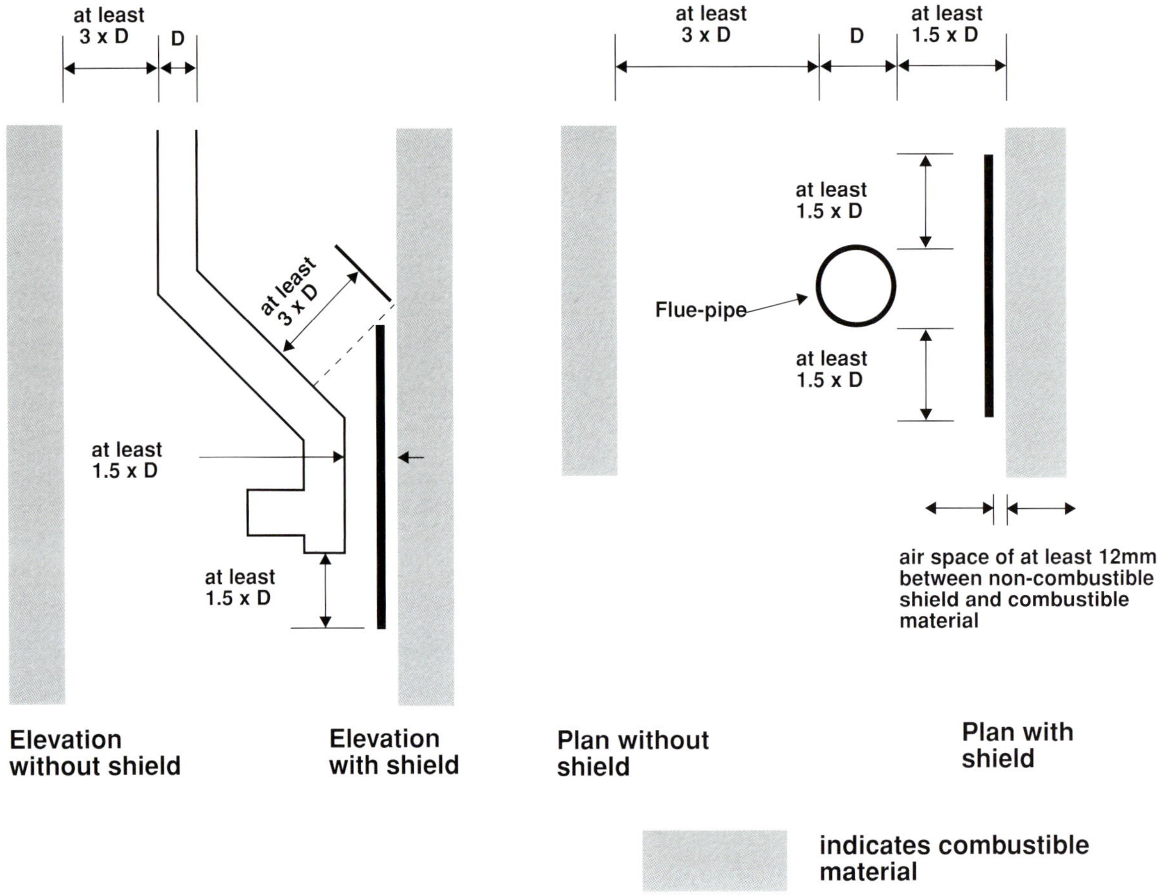

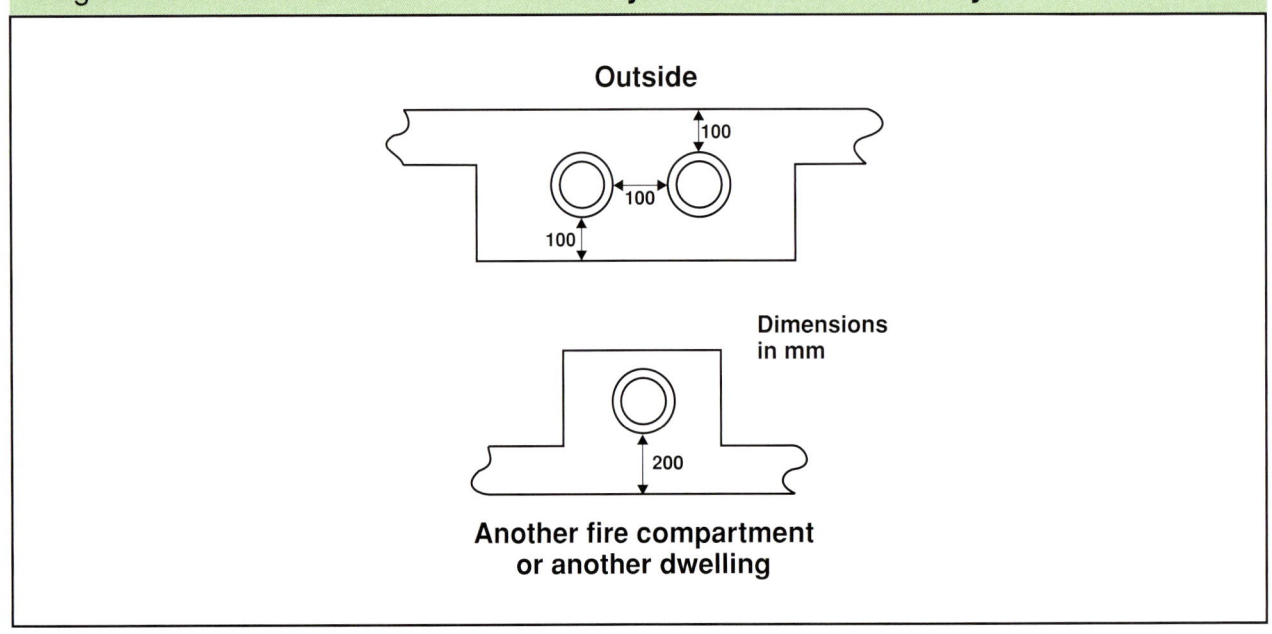

at least 3 x D   D

at least 3 x D   D   at least 1.5 x D

at least 1.5 x D

Flue-pipe

at least 1.5 x D

at least 3 x D

at least 1.5 x D

at least 1.5 x D

air space of at least 12mm between non-combustible shield and combustible material

Elevation without shield

Elevation with shield

Plan without shield

Plan with shield

indicates combustible material

Shields should either:
  a) **extend beyond the fluepipe by at least 1.5 X D; or**
  b) **make any path between fluepipes and combustible material at least 3 X D long**

Diagram 2.4: Wall thicknesses for masonry and flueblock chimneys

Outside

100

100

100

Dimensions in mm

200

Another fire compartment or another dwelling

Diagram 2.5: **Minimum separation distances from combustible material in or near a chimney**

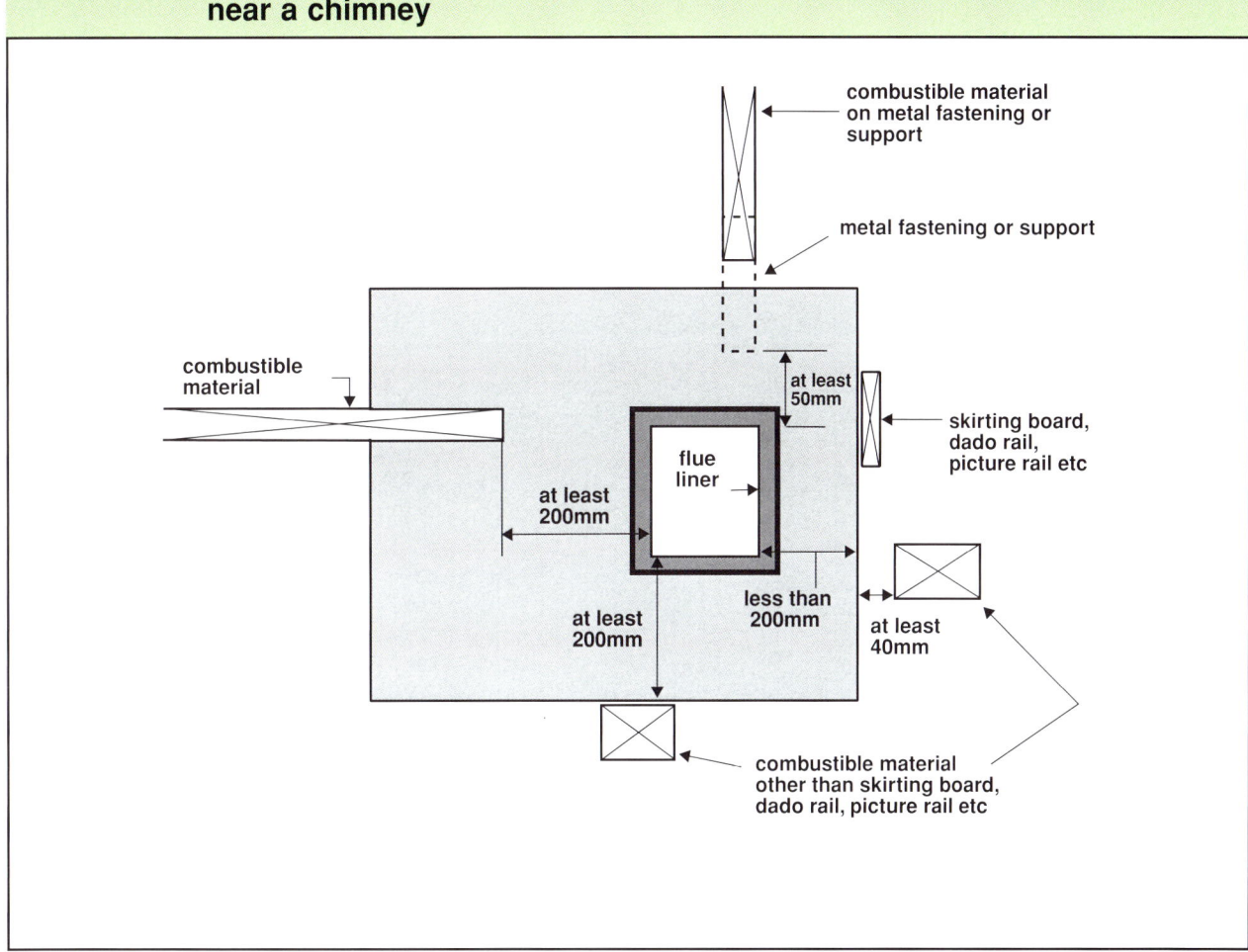

Factory-made metal chimneys

2.19 A way of meeting the requirements would be to comply with Paragraphs 1.42 to 1.46 in Section 1 (but not Paragraph 1.42(b).

Lining and relining of flues in chimneys

2.20 Lining or relining flues may be building work and, in any case, such work should be carried out so that the objectives of J2 to J4 are met (see Paragraphs 1.34 and 1.35). Existing flues being re-used should be checked as described in Paragraph 1.36. Ways of meeting the requirements include the use of:

a)   liners whose performance is independently certified as being at least equal to that corresponding to the designation T450 N2 S D3, as described in BS EN 1443:1999, such as:

    i)   factory-made flue lining systems such as a double skin flexible stainless steel lining which is independently certified as suitable for use with solid fuel burning appliances;

    ii)   a cast *in-situ* flue relining system where the material and installation

    procedures are independently certified as suitable for use with solid fuel burning appliances;

    iii)   other systems which are independently certified as being suitable for use with solid fuel burning appliances and meeting the criteria in (a);

b)   liners as described in Paragraph 1.27.

Formation of gathers

2.21 To minimise resistance to the proper working of flues, tapered gathers should be provided in fireplaces for open fires. Ways of achieving these gathers include:

a)   using prefabricated gather components built into a fireplace recess, as shown in Diagram 2.6(a); or

b)   corbelling of masonry as shown in Diagram 2.6(b); or

c)   using a suitable canopy, as shown in Diagram 2.7; or

d)   using a prefabricated appliance chamber incorporating a gather.

Diagram 2.6: **Construction of fireplace gathers**

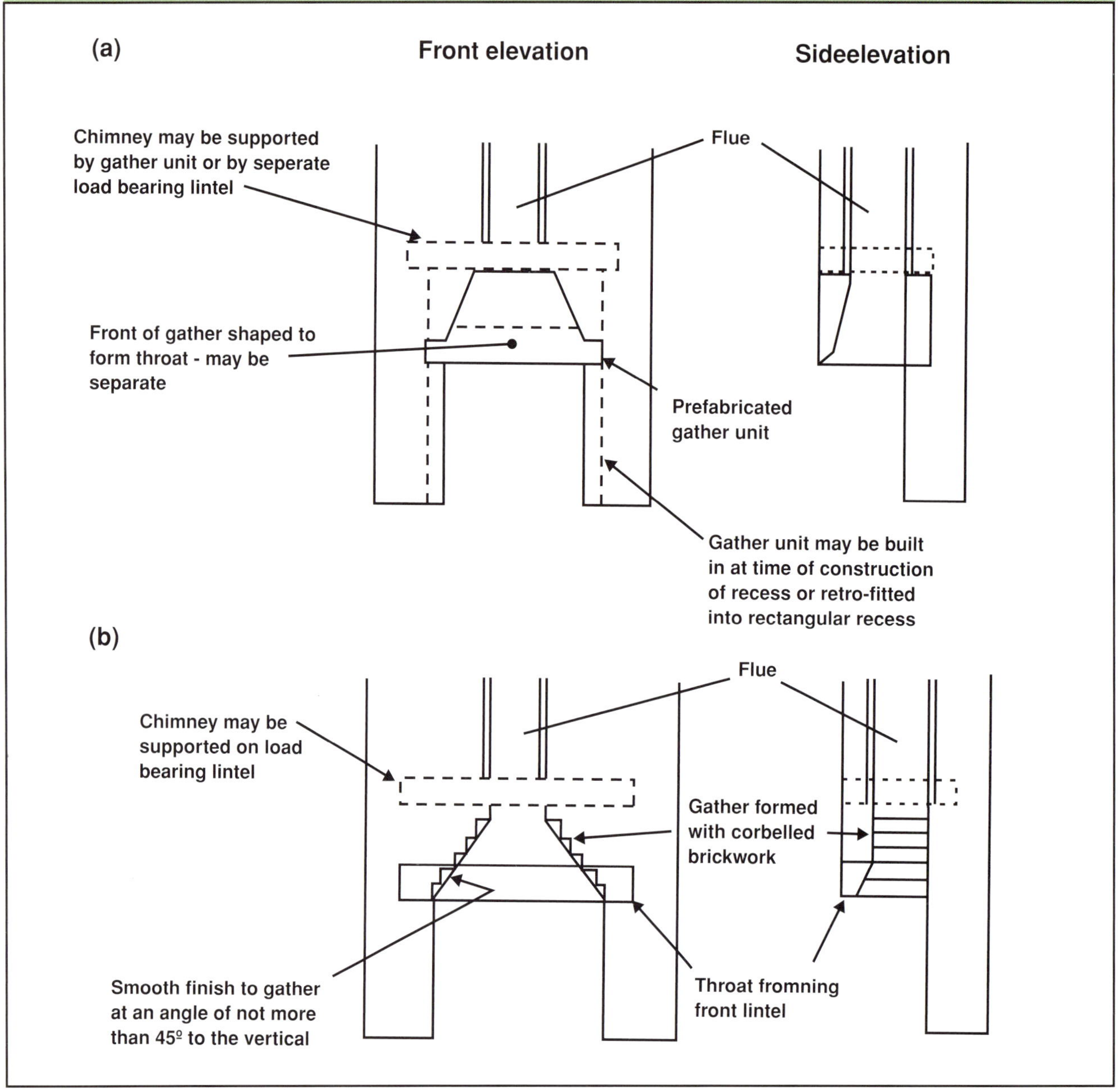

(a)

Front elevation   Sideelevation

Chimney may be supported by gather unit or by seperate load bearing lintel

Flue

Front of gather shaped to form throat - may be separate

Prefabricated gather unit

Gather unit may be built in at time of construction of recess or retro-fitted into rectangular recess

(b)

Flue

Chimney may be supported on load bearing lintel

Gather formed with corbelled brickwork

Smooth finish to gather at an angle of not more than 45º to the vertical

Throat fromning front lintel

Diagram 2.7: **Canopy for an open solid fuel fire**

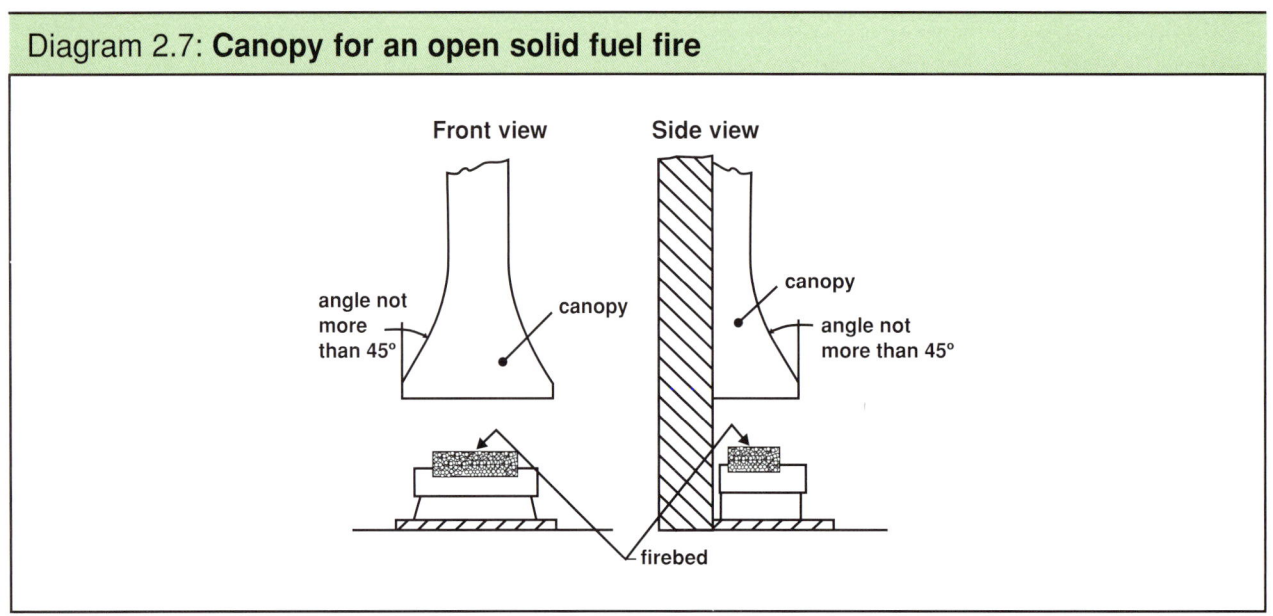

Front view   Side view

angle not more than 45°

canopy

canopy

angle not more than 45°

firebed

Hearths

2.22 Hearths should be constructed of suitably robust materials and to appropriate dimensions such that, in normal use, they prevent combustion appliances setting fire to the building fabric and furnishings, and they limit the risk of people being accidentally burnt. A way of making provision would be adopt the guidance in Paragraphs 2.23 to 2.28 and to provide a hearth appropriate to the temperatures the appliance can create around it. The hearth should be able to accommodate the weight of the appliance and its chimney if the chimney is not independently supported.

2.23 Appliances should stand wholly above:

a)   hearths made of non-combustible board/sheet material or tiles at least 12mm thick, if the appliance is not to stand in an appliance recess and it has been independently certified that it cannot cause the temperature of the hearth to exceed 100°C; or

b)   constructional hearths in accordance with the paragraphs below.

2.24 Constructional hearths should:

a)   have plan dimensions as shown in Diagram 2.8; and

b)   be made of solid, non-combustible material, such as concrete or masonry, at least 125mm thick, including the thickness of any non-combustible floor and/or decorative surface.

Diagram 2.8: Constructional hearth suitable for a solid fuel appliance (including open fires)

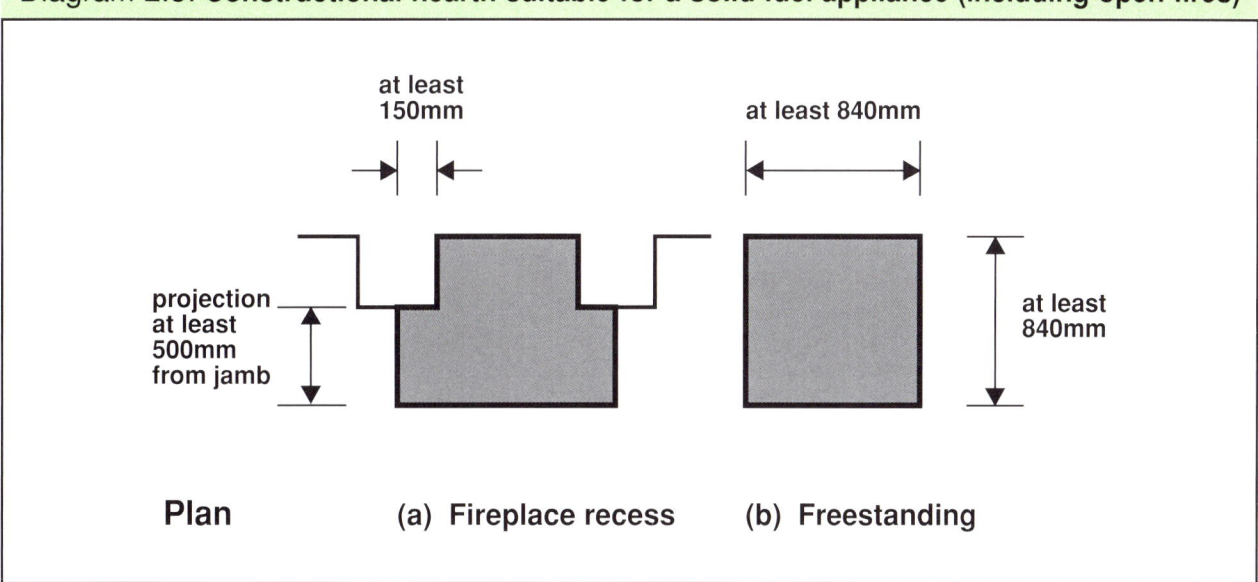

at least 150mm

at least 840mm

projection at least 500mm from jamb

at least 840mm

Plan   **(a) Fireplace recess**   **(b) Freestanding**

Diagram 2.9 : Constructional hearths suitable for solid fuel appliances (including open fires)

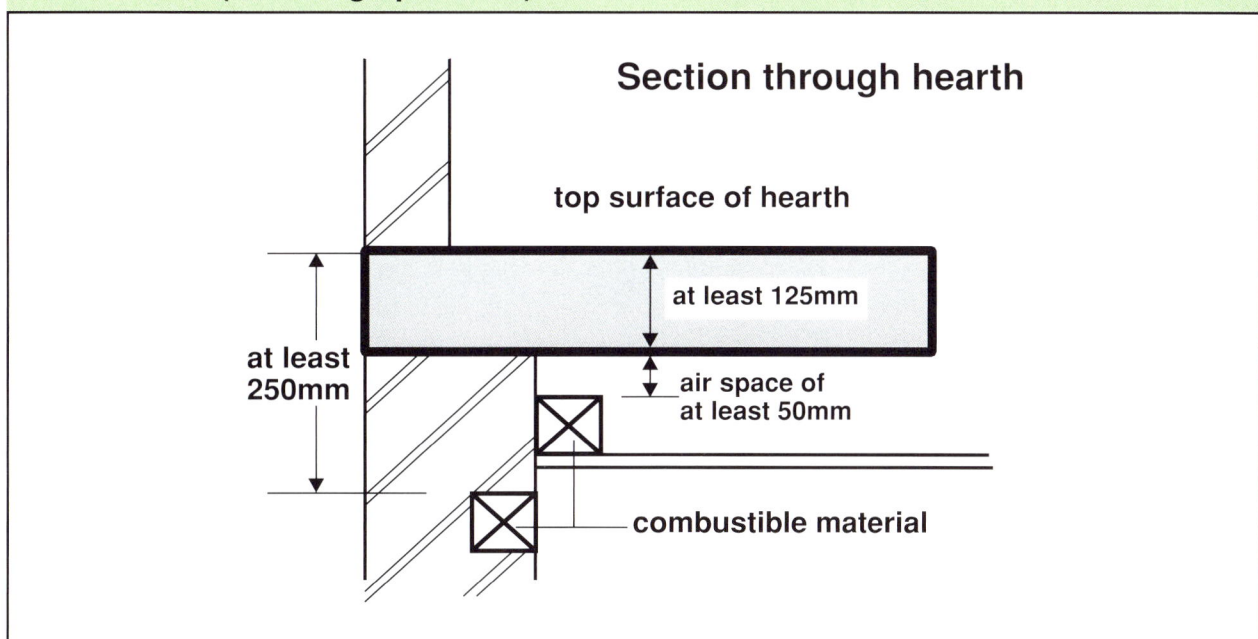

Section through hearth

top surface of hearth

at least 125mm

at least 250mm

air space of at least 50mm

combustible material

Diagram 2.10: Non-combustible hearth surface surrounding a solid fuel appliance

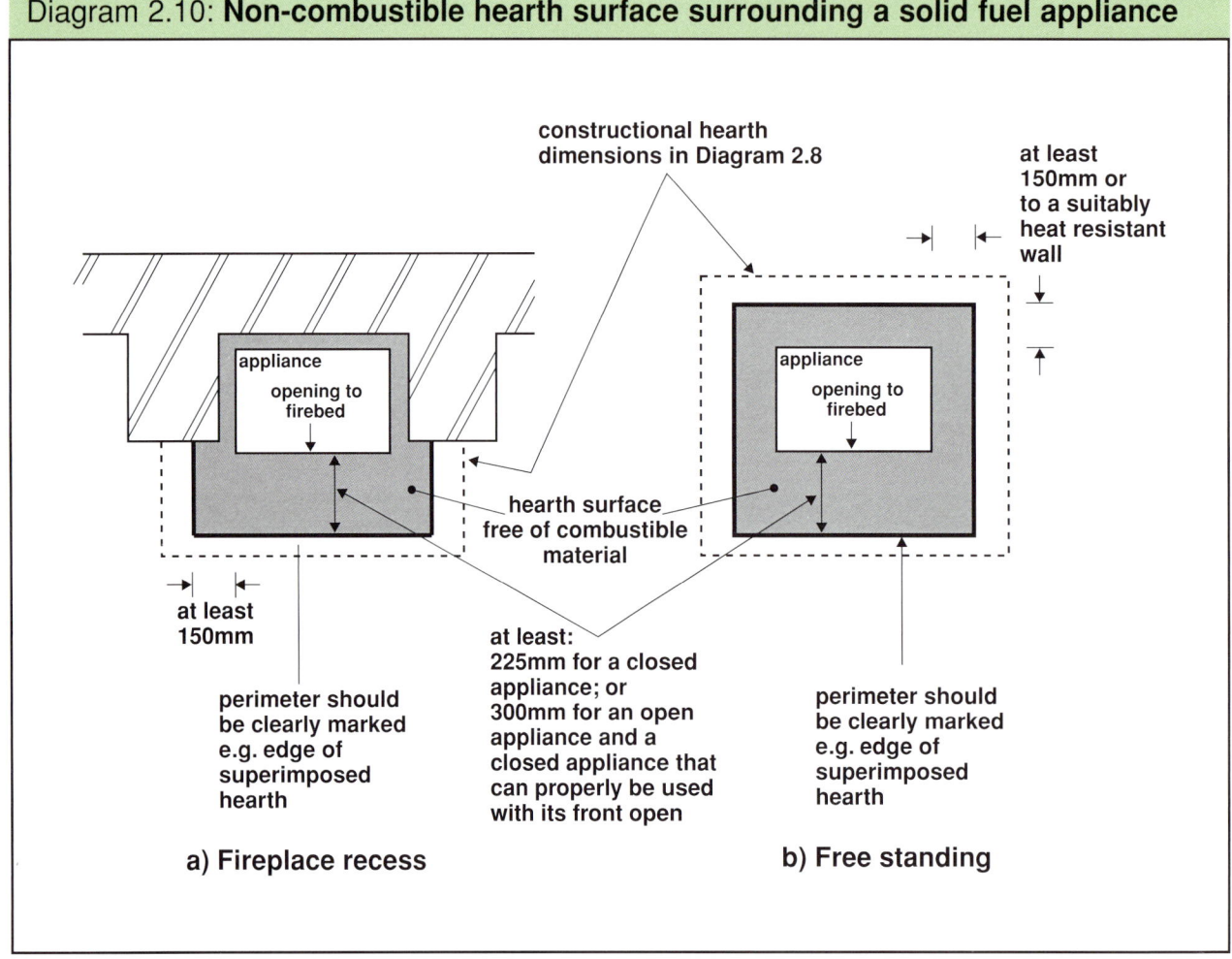

a) **Fireplace recess**

b) **Free standing**

2.25 Combustible material should not be placed beneath constructional hearths unless there is an air-space of at least 50mm between the underside of the hearth and the combustible material, or the combustible material is at least 250mm below the top of the hearth (see Diagram 2.9).

2.26 An appliance should be located on a hearth so that it is surrounded by a surface free of combustible material as shown in Diagram 2.10. This surface may be part of the surface of the hearth provided in accordance with Paragraph 2.23, or it may be the surface of a superimposed hearth laid wholly or partly upon a constructional hearth. The edges of this surface should be marked to provide a warning to the building occupants and to discourage combustible floor finishes such as carpet from being laid too close to the appliance. A way of achieving this would be to provide a change in level.

2.27 Combustible material placed on or beside a constructional hearth should not extend under a superimposed hearth by more than 25mm or to closer than 150mm measured horizontally to the appliance.

2.28 Some ways of making these provisions are shown in Diagram 2.11.

Fireplace recesses and prefabricated appliance chambers

2.29 Fireplaces need to be constructed such that they adequately protect the building fabric from catching fire. A way of achieving the requirements would be to build:

a)   fireplace recesses from masonry or concrete as shown in Diagram 2.12; or

b)   prefabricated factory-made appliance chambers using components that are made of insulating concrete having a density of between 1200 and 1700kg/m^3 and with the minimum thickness as shown in Table 2.3. Components should be supplied as sets for assembly and jointing in accordance with the manufacturer's instructions.

Diagram 2.11: **Ways of providing hearths**

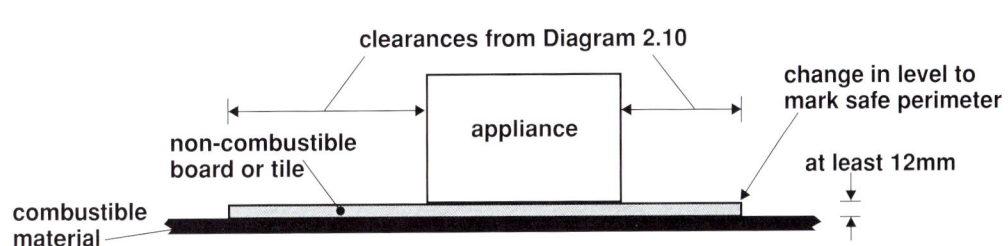

a) **Appliance that cannot cause hearth temperature to exceed 100°C**

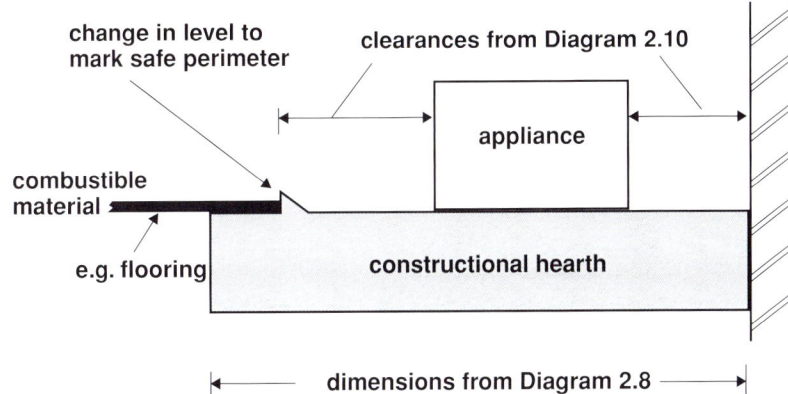

b) **Any appliance standing directly on a constructional hearth**

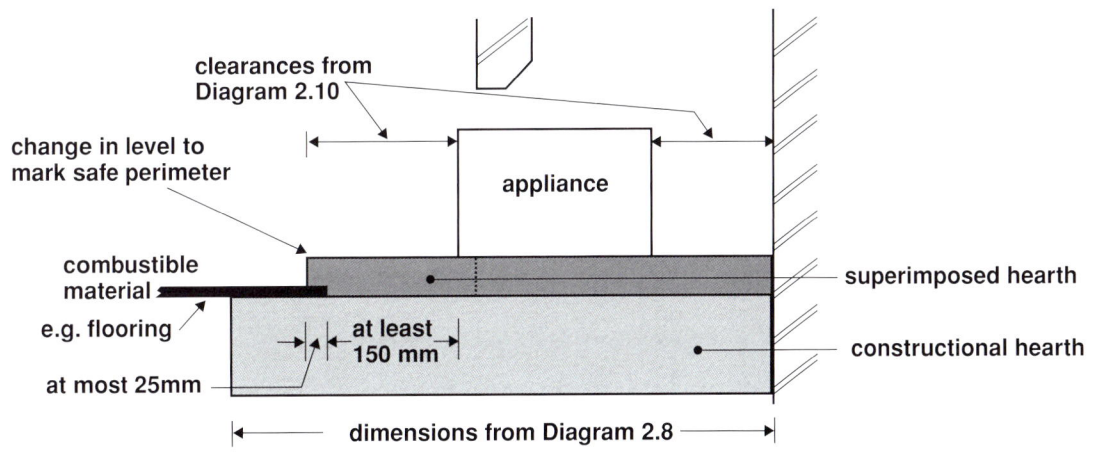

c) **Any appliance in a fireplace recess with a superimposed hearth**

Table 2.3: **Prefabricated appliance chambers: Minimum thickness**

Component	minimum thickness (mm)
base	50
side section, forming wall on either side of chamber	75
back section, forming rear of chamber	100
top slab, lintel or gather, forming top of chamber	100

Diagram 2.12: **Fireplace recesses**

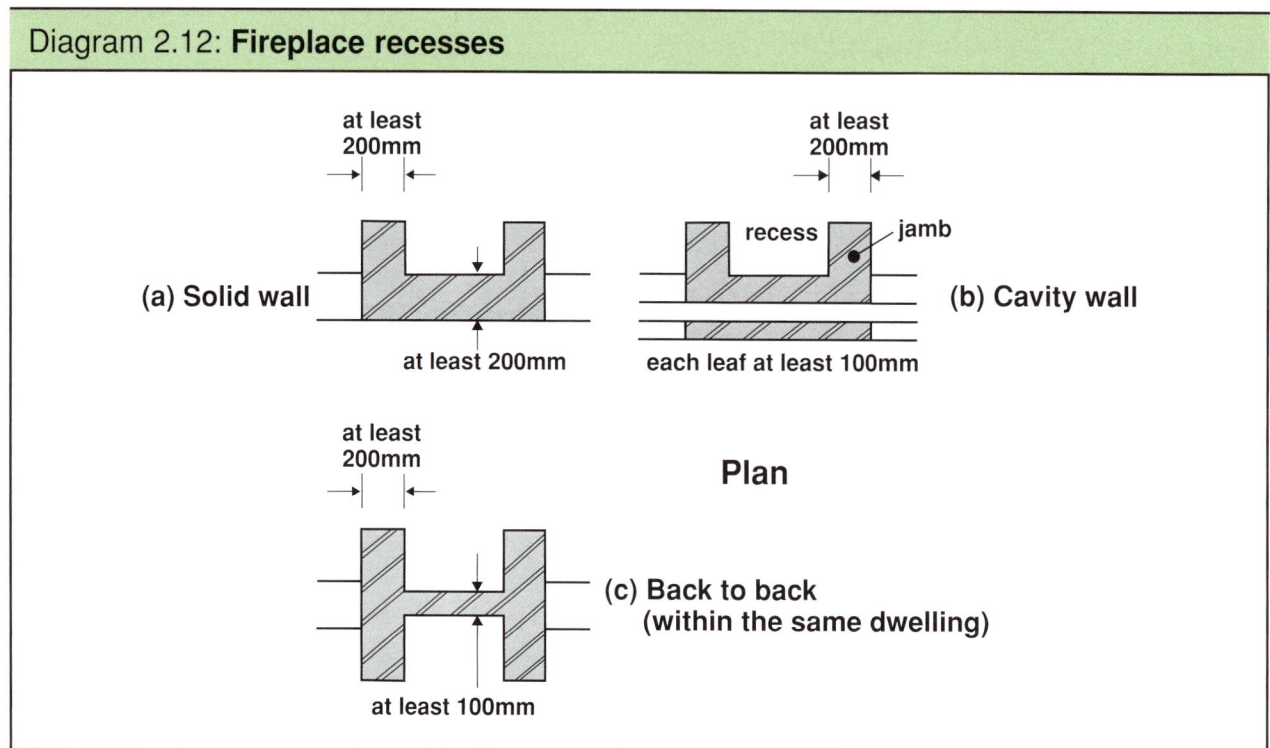

(a) Solid wall — at least 200mm; at least 200mm

(b) Cavity wall — at least 200mm; recess; jamb; each leaf at least 100mm

Plan

(c) Back to back (within the same dwelling) — at least 200mm; at least 100mm

Diagram 2.13: **Open fireplaces: throat and fireplace components**

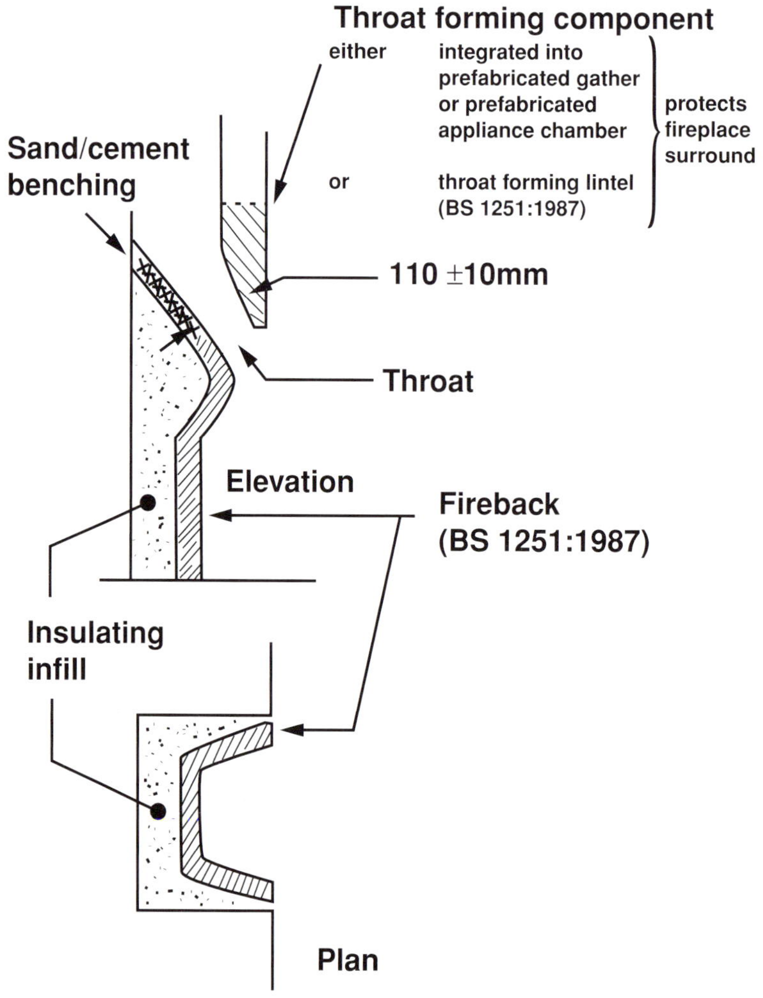

Throat forming component

either: integrated into prefabricated gather or prefabricated appliance chamber

or: throat forming lintel (BS 1251:1987)

protects fireplace surround

110 ±10mm

Sand/cement benching

Throat

Elevation

Fireback (BS 1251:1987)

Insulating infill

Plan

Diagram 2.14: **Walls adjacent to hearths**

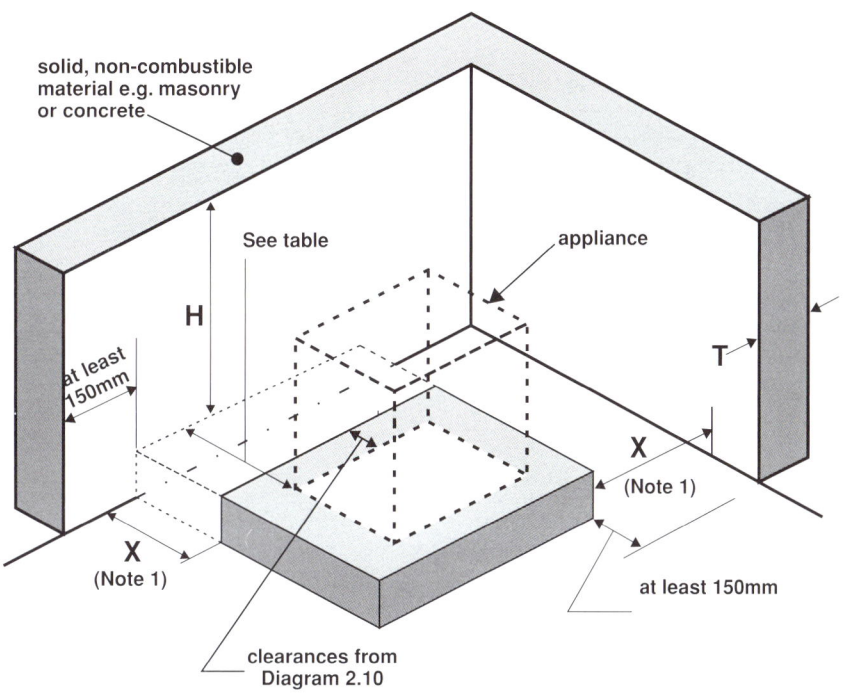

solid, non-combustible material e.g. masonry or concrete

See table

appliance

H

T

at least 150mm

X
(Note 1)

X
(Note 1)

at least 150mm

clearances from Diagram 2.10

Location of hearth or appliance	Solid, non-combustibe material	
	Thickness (T)	Height (H)
where the hearth abuts a wall and the appliance is not more than 50mm from the wall	200mm	at least 300mm above the appliance and 1.2m above the hearth
where the hearth abuts a wall and the appliance is more than 50mm but not more than 300mm from the wall	75mm	at least 300mm above the appliance and 1.2m above the hearth
where the hearth does not abut a wall and is no more than 150mm from the wall (see Note 1)	75mm	at least 1.2m above the hearth
Note: 1. There is no requirement for protection of the wall where X is more than 150mm		

Fireplace lining components

2.30 A fireplace recess may require protection from heat if it is to provide a durable setting for certain appliances such as inset open fires. Suitable protection would be fireplace lining components as shown in Diagram 2.13 or lining the recess with suitable firebricks.

Walls adjacent to hearths

2.31 Walls that are not part of a fireplace recess or a prefabricated appliance chamber but are adjacent to hearths or appliances also need to protect the building from catching fire. A way of achieving the requirement is shown in Diagram 2.14. Thinner material could be used provided it gives the same overall level of protection as the solid non-combustible material.

Alternative approach

The requirements may also be met by adopting the relevant recommendations in the publications listed below to achieve an equivalent level of performance to that obtained by following the guidance in this Approved Document:

a)   BS 6461: Installation of chimneys and flues for domestic appliances burning solid fuel (including wood and peat). Code of practice for masonry chimneys and flue pipes. Part 1: 1984 (1998); and

b)   BS 7566: Installation of factory made chimneys to BS 4543 for domestic appliances Parts 1 to 4: 1992 (1998); and

c)   BS 8303: Installation of domestic heating and cooking appliances burning solid mineral fuels. Parts 1 to 3: 1994.

Section 3

ADDITIONAL PROVISIONS FOR GAS BURNING APPLIANCES WITH A RATED INPUT UP TO 70KW (NET)

Note: This section should be read in conjunction with Sections 0 and 1

Gas Safety (Installation and Use) Regulations

3.1   All combustion installations must be accommodated in ways that meet the requirements of the Building Regulations. However gas installations also have to comply with the Gas Safety (Installation and Use) Regulations which require professional work to be undertaken by a member of a class of persons approved by the Health and Safety Executive (HSE). Because of this, the Building Regulations allow that work need not be notified to Building Control Bodies if it solely comprises the installation of a gas appliance and it is to be undertaken by a member of such an approved class of persons. The Gas Safety (Installation and Use) Regulations cover the safe installation of gas fittings, appliances and flues. The following paragraphs give builders and lay readers an outline of some of the main requirements of the Gas Safety (Installation and Use) Regulations but for further information reference should be made to the Health and Safety Commission's Approved Code of Practice (see below) or Building Control Bodies.

3.2   The Gas Safety (Installation and Use) Regulations require that (a) gas fittings, appliances and gas storage vessels must only be installed by a person with the required competence and (b) any person having control to any extent of gas work must ensure that the person carrying out that work has the required competence and (c) any gas installation businesses, whether an employer or self-employed, must be a member of a class of persons approved by the HSE; for the time being this means they must be registered with CORGI, the Council for Registered Gas Installers.

3.3   Guidance on the individual competency required for gas work is given in the Health and Safety Commission's Approved Code of Practice "Standards of training in safe gas installation". Persons deemed competent to carry out gas work are those who hold a current certificate of competence in the type of activity to be conducted issued under the Approved Code of Practice arrangements, or under a nationally accredited certification scheme.

3.4   The Gas Safety (Installation and Use) Regulations control all aspects of the ways combustion systems fired by gas (including natural gas and LPG) are installed, maintained and used, mainly in domestic and commercial premises, and the classes of persons who may undertake gas work. The Regulations may be amended from time to time and whichever Regulations are currently in force at the time an installation is carried out must be complied with. The advice given below reflects the present state of the Gas Safety (Installation and Use) Regulations following the amendments that came into effect on 31 October 1998.

3.5   The text of the Regulations and guidance on how to comply with them are contained in the Health and Safety Executive (HSE) Approved Code of Practice "Safety in the installation and use of gas systems and appliances". Important elements of the Regulations include that:

a)   any appliance installed in a room used or intended to be used as a bath or shower room must be of the room-sealed type;

b)   a gas fire, other gas space heater or gas water heater of more than 14kW (gross) heat input (12.7kW (net) heat input) must not be installed in a room used or intended to be used as sleeping accommodation unless the appliance is room-sealed;

c)   a gas fire, other space heater or gas water heater of up to 14kW (gross) heat input (12.7kW (net) heat input) must not be installed in a room used or intended to be used as sleeping accommodation unless it is room sealed or equipped with a device designed to shut down the appliance before there is a build-up of a dangerous quantity of the products of combustion in the room concerned;

d)   the restrictions in (a)–(c) above also apply in respect of any cupboard or compartment within the rooms concerned, and to any cupboard, compartment or space adjacent to, and with an air vent into such a room;

e)   instantaneous water heaters (installed in any room) must be room-sealed or have fitted a safety device to shut down the appliance as in (c) above;

f)   precautions must be taken to ensure that all installation pipework, gas fittings, appliances and flues are installed safely. When any gas appliance is installed, checks are required for ensuring compliance with the Regulations, including the effectiveness of the flue, the supply of combustion air, the operating pressure or heat input (or where necessary both), and the operation of the appliance to ensure its safe functioning;

g)   any flue must be installed in a safe position;

h)   no alteration is allowed to any premises in which a gas fitting or gas storage vessel is fitted which would adversely affect the safety of that fitting or vessel, causing it no longer to comply with the Regulations;

i)   LPG storage vessels and LPG fired appliances fitted with automatic ignition devices or pilot lights must not be installed in cellars or basements.

Gas fires (other than flueless gas fires)

3.6 These appliances fall into the main categories shown in Diagram 3.1 and the building provisions for accommodating them safely differ for each type.

3.7 Provided it can be shown to be safe, gas fires may be installed in fireplaces which have flues designed to serve solid fuel appliances. Certain types of gas fire may also be installed in fireplaces which have flues designed specifically for gas appliances. The Gas Appliances (Safety) Regulations 1995 require that particular combinations of appliance, flue box (where required) and flue must be selected from those stated in the manufacturer's instructions as having been shown to be safe by a Notified Body (see Paragraph 0.4 (32)).

Flueless gas appliances

3.8 Flueless appliances should meet the requirements, including requirement J2. A way of achieving this would be to follow the guidance on ventilation provisions for flueless appliances beginning at Paragraph 3.15.

3.9 A flueless instantaneous water heater should not be installed in a room or space having a volume of less than 5m³.

Diagram 3.1: **Types of gas fire**

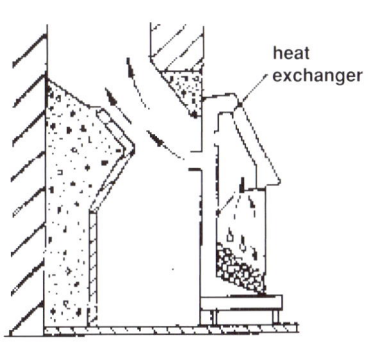

(a) Radiant convector gas fires, convector heaters and fire / back boilers, as described in BS 5871: Part 1

These stand in front of a closure plate which is fitted to the fireplace opening of a fireplace recess or suitable fluebox. The appliance covers the full height of the fireplace opening so that air only enters through purpose designed openings and the flue gases only discharge through the flue spigot.

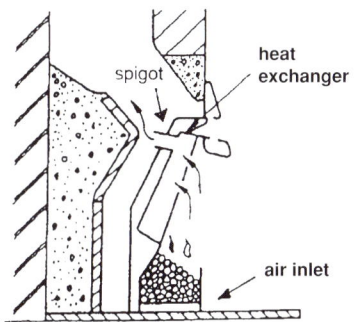

(b) Inset Live Fuel Effect (ILFE) fires, as described in BS 5871: Part 2

These stand fully or partially within a fireplace recess or suitable fluebox and give the impression of an open fire. The appliance covers the full height of the fireplace opening so that air only enters through purpose designed openings and the flue gases only discharge through the spigot.

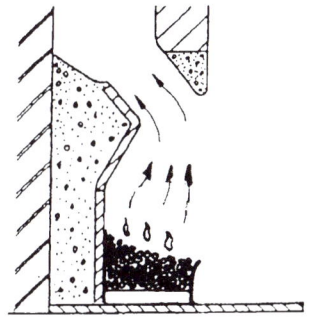

(c) Decorative Fuel Effect (DFE) fires, as described in BS 5871: Part 3

These are gas-fired imitations which can be substituted for the solid fuel appliances in open fires. Where suitable, they can also be used in flueboxes designed for gas appliances only.

Common designs include beds of artificial coals shaped to fit into a fireplace recess or baskets of artificial logs for use in larger fireplaces or under canopies.

Note: For illustration purposes, this diagram shows gas fires installed at or within a fireplace recess formed by fireplace components within a builders opening. The actual setting for an appliance depends upon its type and manufacturer's installation instructions.

Air supply to gas fires and other appliances

3.10 A way of meeting the requirements would be to follow the general guidance given in Section 1, beginning at Paragraph 1.2, in conjunction with the guidance below.

Flued Decorative Fuel Effect (DFE) fires

3.11 Any room or space intended to contain a DFE fire should have permanently open air vents as described in (a) or (b) below, unless the installation is in accordance with Paragraph 3.12:

a)   for a DFE fire in a fireplace recess with a throat, the air vent free area should be at least 10,000mm^2 (100cm^2);

b)   for a DFE fire in a fireplace with no throat, such as a fire under a canopy, the air vent free area should be sized in accordance with Section 2 of this Approved Document, as if the room were intended to contain a solid fuel fire (see Table 2.1).

3.12 Permanently open air vents may not be necessary for DFE fires with ratings not exceeding 7kW (net) that have been independently certified by a Notified Body as having a flue gas clearance rate (without spilling) not exceeding 70m^3/hour (see Paragraph 0.4 (32)).

Flued appliances other than Decorative Fuel Effect fires

3.13 These appliances include inset live fuel effect (ILFE) fires, radiant convector fires and boilers, in both room-sealed and open-flued variants.

3.14 A way of meeting the requirement would be to follow the guidance in Diagram 3.2. An example calculation illustrating the use of this guidance is given in Appendix C.

Air supply to flueless appliances

3.15 For some flueless appliances, it may be necessary to provide permanently open air vents and/or make provision for rapid ventilation as recommended in BS 5440-2: 2000 or equivalent, to comply with Part F as well as Part J of the Building Regulations. Some ways of meeting the requirement when installing flueless cookers (including ovens, grills or hotplates) flueless water heaters and flueless space heaters, are given in Diagram 3.3.

3.16 A room containing a gas point intended for use with a flueless appliance (such as a gas point for a cooker or a gas point for a space or water heater, the gas point not being adjacent to a flue) should have the ventilation provision required for the installation of that appliance (calculated on the basis that an appliance with the largest rating consistent with the table to Diagram 3.3 could be installed there).

Size of natural draught flues for open flued appliances

3.17 Where builders wish to provide (or refurbish) flues for gas appliances but do not intend to supply the appliances, a way of showing compliance would be to size flues in accordance with Table 3.1.

3.18 If an existing flue is to be used it should be checked in accordance with Paragraph 1.36.

3.19 For appliances that are CE marked as compliant with the Gas Appliances (Safety) Regulations, flues should be sized in accordance with the manufacturer's installation instructions.

3.20 Connecting fluepipes should be the same size in terms of diameter and/or equivalent cross sectional area as the appliance flue outlet. The chimney flue should have at least the same cross sectional area as that of the appliance flue outlet.

Table 3.1: **Size of flues for gas fired appliances**

Intended installation	Minimum flue size		
Radiant / Convector gas fire	New flue: Circular Rectangular	 125mm diameter 16,500mm^2 cross sectional area with a minimum dimension of 90mm	
	Existing flue: Circular Rectangular	 125mm diameter 12,000mm^2 cross sectional area with a minimum dimension of 63mm	
ILFE fire or DFE fire within a fireplace opening up to 500mm x 550mm	Circular or Rectangular	Minimum flue dimension of 175mm (1)	
DFE fire installed in a fireplace with an opening in excess of 500mm x 550mm	Calculate in accordance with Paragraph 2.7 in Section 2		

Note:

1. Some ILFE and DFE appliances require a circular flue of at least 125mm diameter

Diagram 3.2: Free areas of permanently open air vents for gas appliance installations (other than decorative fuel effect fires or flueless appliances)

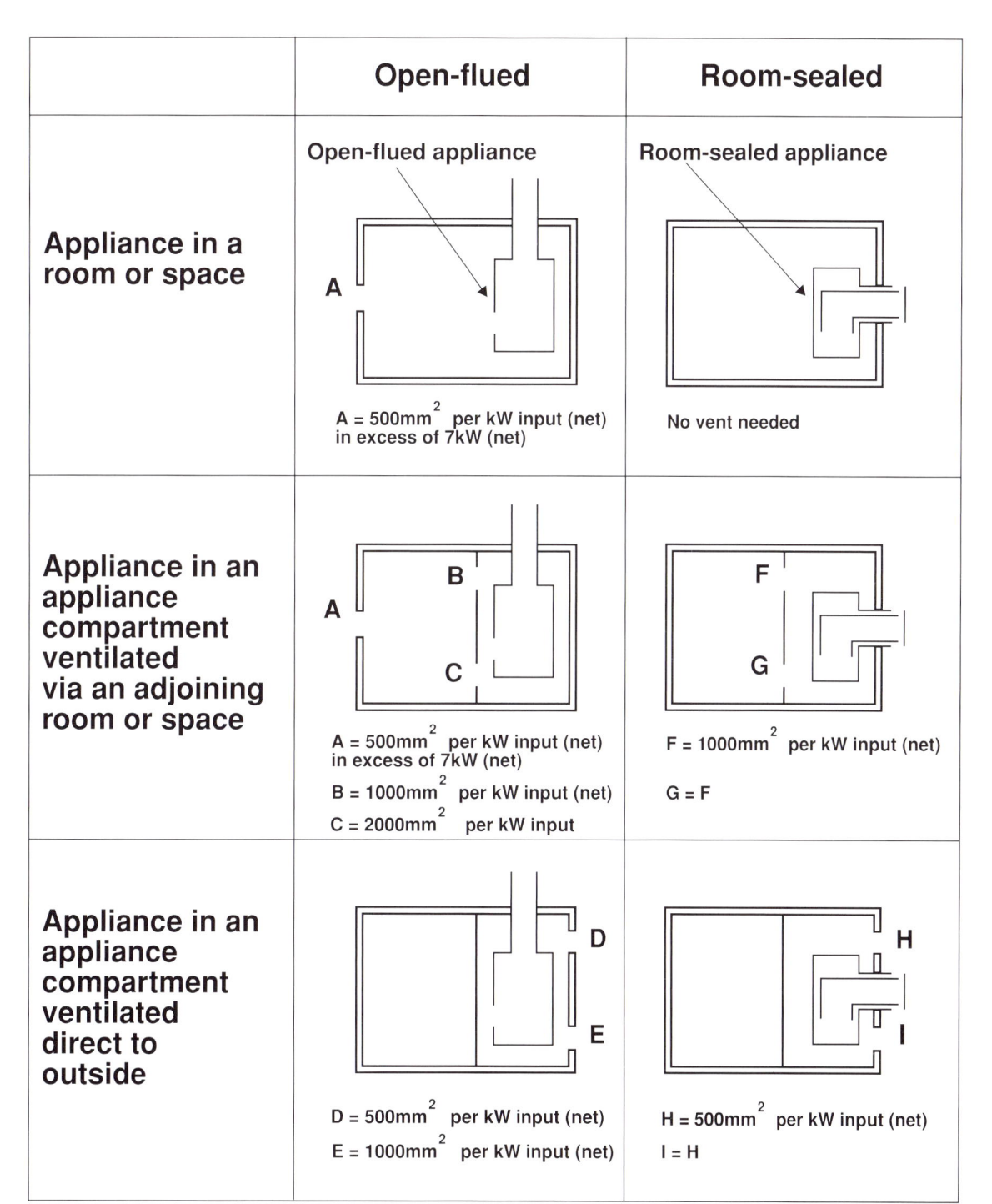

	Open-flued	Room-sealed
Appliance in a room or space	Open-flued appliance A $A = 500mm^2$ per kW input (net) in excess of 7kW (net)	Room-sealed appliance No vent needed
Appliance in an appliance compartment ventilated via an adjoining room or space	A B C $A = 500mm^2$ per kW input (net) in excess of 7kW (net) $B = 1000mm^2$ per kW input (net) $C = 2000mm^2$ per kW input	F G $F = 1000mm^2$ per kW input (net) $G = F$
Appliance in an appliance compartment ventilated direct to outside	D E $D = 500mm^2$ per kW input (net) $E = 1000mm^2$ per kW input (net)	H I $H = 500mm^2$ per kW input (net) $I = H$

Notes:

1. A,D,E,D and I are permanently open vents on the outside. B, C, F and G are permanently open vents between an appliance compartment and a room or a space.

2. Calculations employ the appliance rated net heat input as described in Paragraph 0.4 (35).

3. The area given above is the free area of the vent(s) or the equivalent free area for ventilators of more complex design.

4. Divide the area given above in mm^2 by 100 to find the corresponding area in cm^2.

Diagram 3.3: **Ventilation for flueless gas appliances**

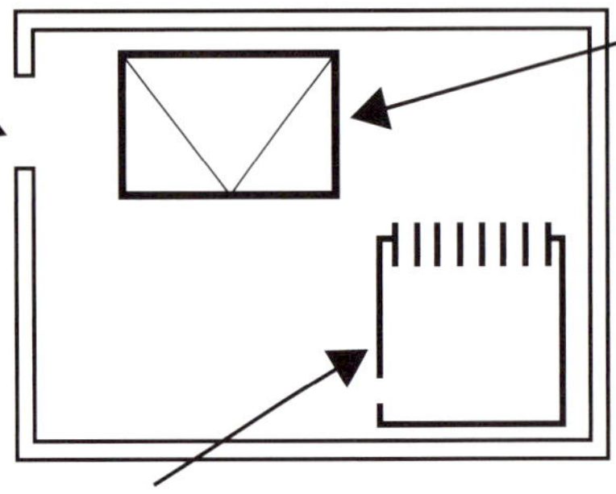

Permanently open vent opening directly to outside with free area not less than that given in Column 4 of the table below

In accordance with Approved Document F:-

a) Openable window, door or similar form of controllable ventilation opening directly to outside;

or

b) for a kitchen, mechanical extract ventilation

Flueless appliance with a rating not exceeding that given in Column 2 of the table below

Free areas of permanently open air vents			
Flueless appliance type	Maximum appliance rated heat input	Volume of room, space or internal space (m^3)	Free area of permanently open air vent (mm^2) (3, 4)
Cooker, oven hotplate or grill or combination thereof	not applicable	<5 5 to 10 >10	10,000 5000 (5) no permanently open vent needed
Instantaneous water heater	11kW(net)	5 to 10 10 to 20 >20	10,000 5000 no permanently open vent needed
Space heater not in an internal space (3, 4)	0.045kW(net) per m^3 volume of room or space[6]	all cases	10,000 PLUS 5500 per kW input (net) in excess of 2.7kW (net)
Space heater in an internal space (3, 4)	0.090kW(net) per m^3 volume of internal space	all cases	10,000 PLUS 2750 perkW input (net) in excess of 5.4kW (net) (7)

Notes:

1. The permanent ventilation provisions listed in this table are additional to the openable elements or (for kitchens only) extract ventilation in accordance with Approved Document F.

2. Divide the area given above in mm^2 by 100 to find the corresponding area in cm^2.

3. An internal space here means one which communicates with several other rooms or spaces. An example would be a hallway or landing.

4. For LPG fired space heaters conforming to BS EN 449:1997, follow the guidance in BS 5440-2:2000.

5. No permanently open vent is needed if the room or space has a door direct to outside.

6. Example: for a space heater in a lounge measuring 4m x 4m x 2.4m (= $38.4m^3$), the appliance rated input should not exceed 38.4 x 0.045 = 1.73kW (net).

7. Example: a hallway containing a space heater with a rated input of 7kW (net) should have a permanently open vent with free area of: 10,000 + 2750 x (7 - 5.4) = 14,400 mm^2.

Height of natural draught flues for open flued appliances

3.21 Flues should be high enough to ensure sufficient draught to safely clear the products of combustion. The height necessary for this will depend upon the type of appliance, the building height, the type of flue and the number of bends in it, and a careful assessment of local wind patterns. For appliances that are CE-marked as compliant with the Gas Appliances (Safety) Regulations, compliance with the manufacturer's installation instructions will meet the requirements.

3.22 Where an older appliance that is not CE marked is to be installed, a way of showing compliance if it has manufacturer's installation instructions would be:

a) for decorative fuel effect fires, to follow the guidance in BS 5871-3:2001; or

b) for appliances other than decorative fuel effect fires, to follow the calculation procedures in BS 5440-1:2000.

Outlets from flues

3.23 Outlets from flues should be so situated externally as to allow the dispersal of products of combustion and, if a balanced flue, the intake of air. A way of meeting this requirement would be to locate flue outlets as shown in Diagram 3.4 and Diagram 3.5.

3.24 Flue outlets should be protected where flues are at significant risk of blockage. Guidance on meeting this requirement is given below.

3.25 Flues serving natural draught open-flued appliances should be fitted with outlet terminals if the flue diameter is no greater than 170mm. Suitable terminals include those complying with BS 715:1993, and BS 1289-1:1986. The risk of blockage of flues of more than 170mm diameter should be assessed in the light of local conditions. In areas where nests of squirrels or jackdaws are likely, the fitting of a protective cage designed for solid fuel use and having a mesh size no larger than 25mm (but no smaller than 6mm) may be an acceptable provision if the total free area of its outlet openings is at least twice the cross sectional area of the flue.

3.26 A flue outlet should be protected with a guard if persons could come into contact with it or if it could be damaged. If a flue outlet is in a vulnerable position, such as where the flue discharges within reach from the ground, or a balcony, veranda or a window, it should be designed to prevent the entry of any matter that could obstruct the flow of flue gases.

Table 3.2: Minimum performance designations for chimney and fluepipe components for use with new gas appliances

Appliance type		Minimum designation (See Notes)
Boiler: open-flued	natural draught	T250 N2 O D 1
	fanned draught	T250 P2 O D 1
	condensing	T250 P2 O W 1
Boiler: room-sealed	natural draught	T250 N2 O D 1
	fanned draught	T250 P2 O D 1
Gas fire - Radiant/convector, ILFE or DFE		T300 N2 O D 1
Air heater	natural draught	T250 N2 O D 1
	fanned draught	T200 P2 O D 1
	SE - duct	T450 N2 O D 1

Notes:

1. The designation of chimney products is described in Paragraph 0.4(9). The BS EN for the product will specify its full designation and marking requirements.

2. These are default designations. Where appliance manufacturer's installation instructions specify a higher designation, this should be complied with.

Provision of flues

3.27 Satisfactory provision of chimneys and fluepipes for gas appliances may by achieved by:

a) following the guidance on the selection of components and the manner of their installation as given in Paragraphs 3.28 to 3.35 below and the references to Section 1;

or (if the intended appliance is new and of known type)

b) i) using factory-made components that have been independently certified as achieving a performance at least equal to that corresponding to the designation given in Table 3.2 for the intended appliance type when tested to an appropriate European chimney standard (BS EN); and

ii) installing these components in accordance with the guidance in Paragraphs 3.28 to 3.35. and Section 1, as relevant, and in accordance with the appliance manufacturer's and component manufacturer's installation instructions.

Connecting fluepipe components

3.28 Satisfactory components for connecting fluepipes include:

a) any of the options in Paragraph 1.32; or

b) sheet metal fluepipes as described in BS 715:1993; or

c) fibre cement pipes as described in BS 7435-1:1991 (1998) or BS 7435-2:1991 (1998); or

d) any other material or component that has been independently certified as suitable for this purpose.

Diagram 3.4: **Location of outlets from flues serving gas appliances**

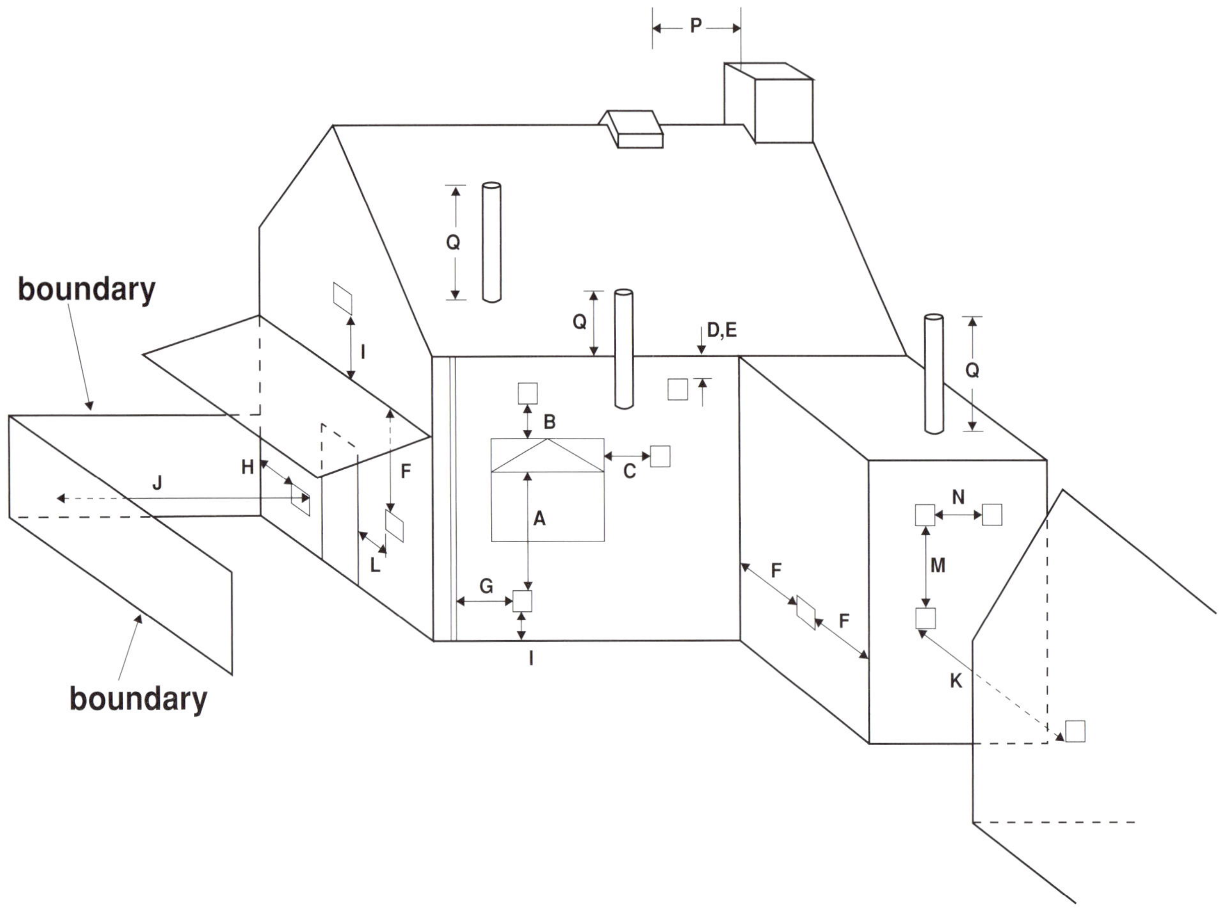

see adjacent table to diagram 3.4
for key to distances

Masonry chimneys

3.29 Masonry chimneys should be built in accordance with Paragraphs 1.27 and 1.28 in Section 1.

Flueblock chimneys

3.30 Chimneys can be constructed from factory-made flueblock systems primarily designed for solid fuel, as described in Paragraphs 1.29 and 1.30 in Section 1. They can also be constructed from factory-made flueblock systems comprising straight blocks, recess units, lintel blocks, offset blocks, transfer blocks and jointing materials complying with:

a)   BS 1289-1:1986 for concrete flueblocks; or

b)   BS EN 1806:2000 for clay/ceramic flueblocks with a performance class of at least FB4 N2.

3.31 Flueblock chimneys should be installed with sealed joints in accordance with the flueblock manufacturer's installation instructions. Where bends or offsets are required, these should be formed using matching factory-made components. Flueblocks which are not intended to be bonded into surrounding masonry should be supported and restrained in accordance with the manufacturer's installation instructions.

Factory-made metal chimneys

3.32 Chimneys for gas appliances may be constructed using systems described in Paragraphs 1.42 to 1.46 in Section 1. Factory-made metal chimneys should be guarded if they could be at risk of damage or the burn hazard they present to people is not immediately apparent.

Table to Diagram 3.4: **Location of outlets from flues serving gas appliances**

Minimum separation distances for terminals in mm

Location		Balanced flue			Open flue	
		Natural draught		Fanned draught	Natural draught	Fanned draught
A	Below an opening (1)	Appliance rated heat input (net)		300	(3)	300
		0 – 7kW >7 – 14kW >14 – 32kW >32kW	300 600 1500 2000			
B	Above an opening (1)	0 – 32kW > 32kW	300 600	300	(3)	300
C	Horizontally to an opening (1)	0 – 7kW >7 – 14kW >14kW	300 400 600	300	(3)	300
D	Below gutters, soil pipes or drain pipes	300		75	(3)	75
E	Below eaves	300		200	(3)	200
F	Below balcony or car port roof	600		200	(3)	200
G	From a vertical drain pipe or soil pipe	300		150 (4)	(3)	150
H	From an internal or external corner or to a boundary alongside the terminal (2)	600		300	(3)	200
I	Above ground, roof or balcony level	300		300	(3)	300
J	From a surface or a boundary facing the terminal (2)	600		600	(3)	600
K	From a terminal facing the terminal	600		1200	(3)	1200
L	From an opening in the car port into the building	1200		1200	(3)	1200
M	Vertically from a terminal on the same wall	1200		1500	(3)	1500
N	Horizontally from a terminal on the same wall	300		300	(3)	300
P	From a structure on the roof	N/A		N/A	1500mm if a ridge terminal. For any other terminal, as given in BS 5440-1:2000	N/A
Q	Above the highest point of intersection with the roof	N/A		Site in accordance with manufacturer's instructions	Site in accordance with BS 5440-1:2000	150

Notes:

1. An opening here means an openable element, such as an openable window, or a fixed opening such as an air vent. However, in addition, the outlet should not be nearer than 150mm (fanned draught) or 300mm (natural draught) to an opening into the building fabric formed for the purpose of accommodating a built in element, such as a window frame.

2. Boundary as defined in Paragraph 0.4 (4). Smaller separations to the boundary may be acceptable for appliances that have been shown to operate safely with such separations from surfaces adjacent to or opposite the flue outlet.

3. Should not be used.

4. This dimension may be reduced to 75mm for appliances of up to 5kW input (net).

5. N/A means not applicable.

Diagram 3.5: **Location of outlets near roof windows from flues serving gas appliances**

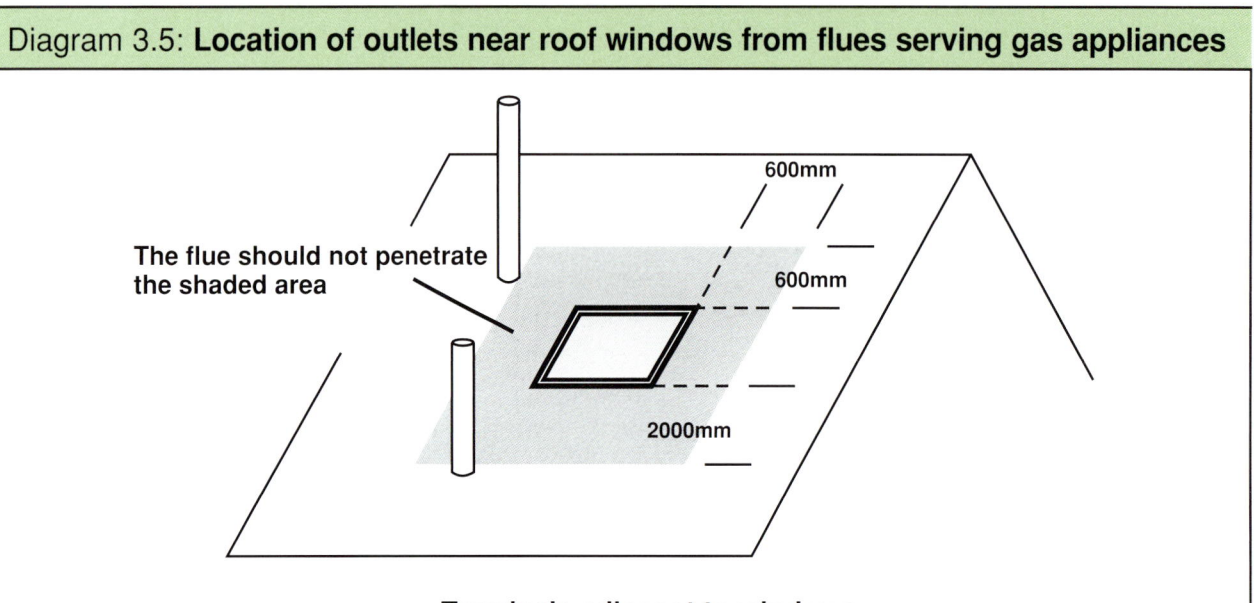

The flue should not penetrate the shaded area

600mm

600mm

2000mm

**Terminals adjacent to windows
or openings on pitched and flat roofs**

Table 3.3: **Protecting buildings from hot flues**

Flue within:	Protection measures
Connecting fluepipe	Flues should be at least 25mm from any combustible material (measured from the outer surface of the flue wall, or the outer surface of the inner wall in the case of multi-walled products). Where passing through a combustible wall, floor or roof (other than a compartment wall floor or roof) this separation can be achieved by a non-combustible sleeve enclosing the fluepipe or chimney with a 25mm airspace to the relevant flue wall. (The airspace could be wholly or partially filled with non-combustible insulating material).
Factory-made chimney complying with BS 715:1993	
Factory-made chimney complying with BS 4543-1:1990 (1996),* BS 4543-2:1990 (1996), and BS 4543-3:1990 (1996)	Install in accordance with Paragraph 1.45 of this Approved Document.
Masonry chimney	Provide at least 25mm of masonry between flues and any combustible material.
Flueblock chimney	Provide flueblock walls at least 25mm thick.

* BS 4543-1:1990 (1996) withdrawn April 2000; partially superseded by BS EN 1859:2000.

Location and shielding of flues

3.33 Combustible materials in the building fabric should be protected from the heat dissipation from flues so that they are not at risk of catching fire. A way of meeting the requirement would be to follow the guidance in Table 3.3.

3.34 Where a fluepipe or chimney penetrates a fire compartment wall or floor, it must not breach the fire separation requirements of Part B. See Approved Document B for more guidance.

3.35 Connecting fluepipes and factory-made chimneys should also be guarded if they could be at risk of damage or if they present a burn hazard to people that is not immediately apparent.

Relining of flues in chimneys

3.36 Lining or relining flues may be building work and in any case, such work should be carried out so that the objectives of requirements J2 to J4 are met (see Paragraphs 1.34 and 1.35). Existing flues being re-used should be checked as described in Paragraph 1.36. For flue liners serving gas appliances, ways of meeting the requirements include the use of:

a)   liners as described in Paragraph 1.27;

b)   liners as described in Paragraph 2.20;

c)   flexible stainless steel liners independently certified as complying with BS 715:1993;

d)   other systems which have been independently certified as suitable for the purpose.

3.37 Flexible metal flue liners should be installed in one complete length without joints within the chimney. Other than for sealing at the top and the bottom, the space between the chimney and the liner should be left empty unless this is contrary to the manufacturer's instructions. Double skin flexible flue liners should be installed in accordance with manufacturer's installation instructions. BS 715 liners should be installed in accordance with BS 5440-1:2000.

Diagram 3.6: Bases for back boilers (installation using a proprietary back boiler enclosure shown)

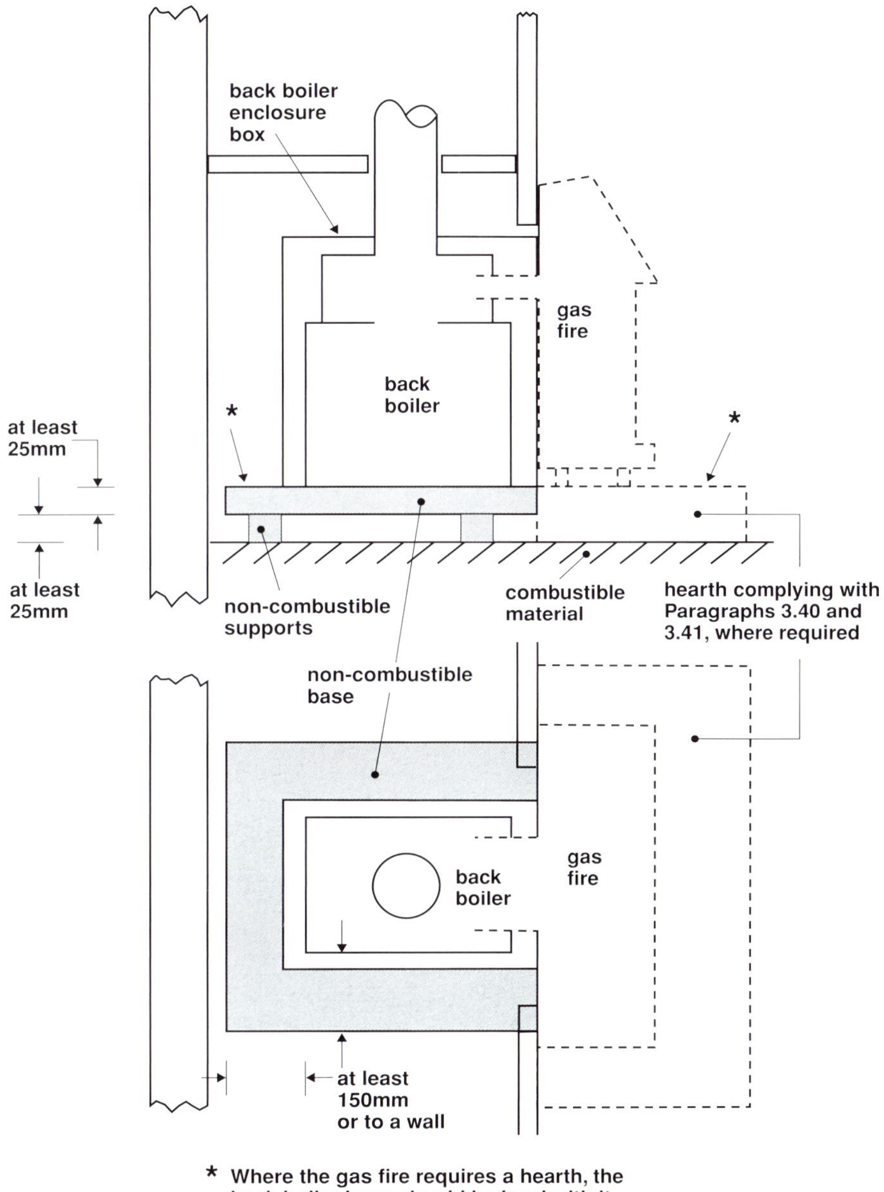

back boiler enclosure box

gas fire

back boiler

at least 25mm

at least 25mm

non-combustible supports

non-combustible base

combustible material

hearth complying with Paragraphs 3.40 and 3.41, where required

back boiler

gas fire

at least 150mm or to a wall

* Where the gas fire requires a hearth, the back boiler base should be level with it

Debris collection space for chimneys

3.38 A debris collection space should be provided at the base of a flue unless it is lined, or constructed of flue blocks, or is a factory-made metal chimney with a flue box. This can be achieved by providing a space having a volume of not less than 12 litres and a depth of at least 250mm below the point where flue gases discharge into the chimney. The space should be readily accessible for clearance of debris, for example by removal of the appliance. For gas fires of the type illustrated in Diagram 3.1 (a) and (b), there should be at least 50mm clearance between the end of the appliance flue outlet and any surface.

Bases for back boilers

3.39 Provisions for back boilers should adequately protect the fabric of the building from heat. A way of meeting the requirement would be to stand back boilers on hearths intended for solid fuel appliances. Alternatively, unless otherwise stated in appliance manufacturer's instructions, a way of meeting the requirements would be to stand back boilers on bases complying with Diagram 3.6.

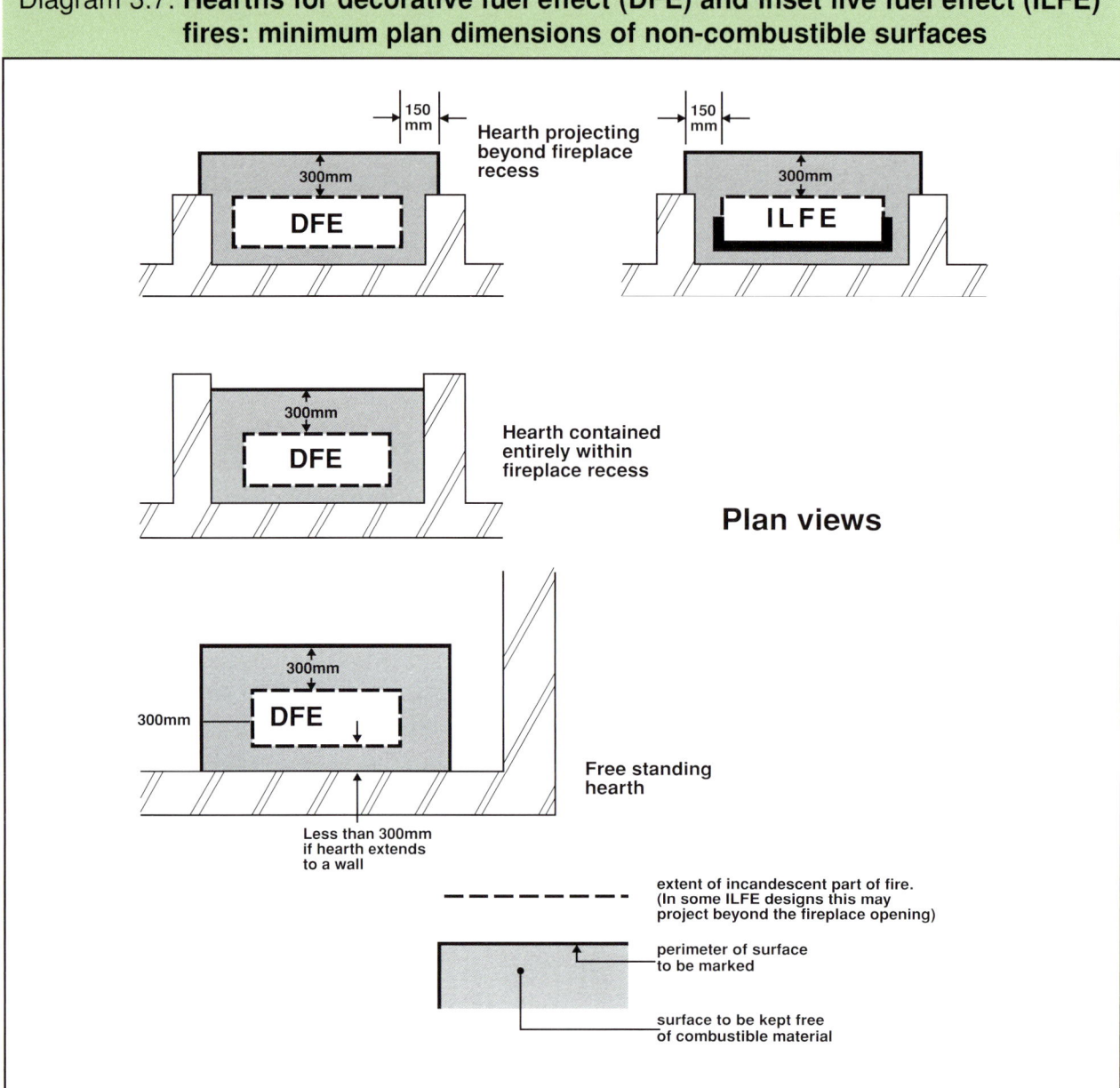

Diagram 3.7: **Hearths for decorative fuel effect (DFE) and inset live fuel effect (ILFE) fires: minimum plan dimensions of non-combustible surfaces**

Hearths

3.40 Appliances should be placed on hearths unless:

a) they are to be installed so that every part of any flame or incandescent material will be at least 225mm above the floor; or

b) the manufacturer's instructions state that a hearth is not required.

3.41 Where hearths are required, guidance on their minimum plan dimensions is given in Diagrams 3.7 and 3.8. Hearths should comprise at least a (top) layer of non-combustible, non-friable material not less than 12mm thick. The edges of hearths should be marked to provide a warning to the building occupants and to discourage combustible floor finishes such as carpet from being laid too close to the appliance. A way of achieving this would be to provide a change in level.

Shielding of appliances

3.42 Gas fired appliances should be located where accidental contact is unlikely and surrounded by a non-combustible surface which provides adequate separation from combustible materials. For appliances that are CE marked as compliant with the Gas Appliances (Safety) Regulations, a way of meeting the requirement would be to adopt the manufacturer's instructions. An alternative approach would be to protect combustible fabric with:

a) a shield of non-combustible material, such as insulating board, with a fire resistant surface; or

b) an air space of at least 75mm (see Diagram 3.9).

Diagram 3.8: **Hearths for other appliances: plan dimensions of non-combustible surfaces**

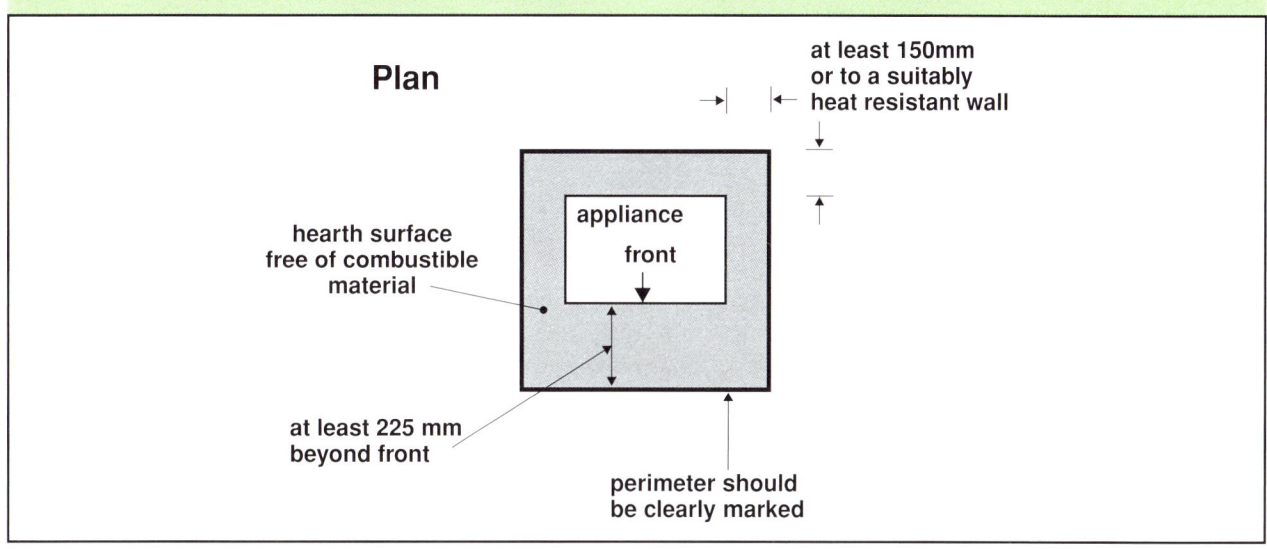

Diagram 3.9: **Shielding of appliances**

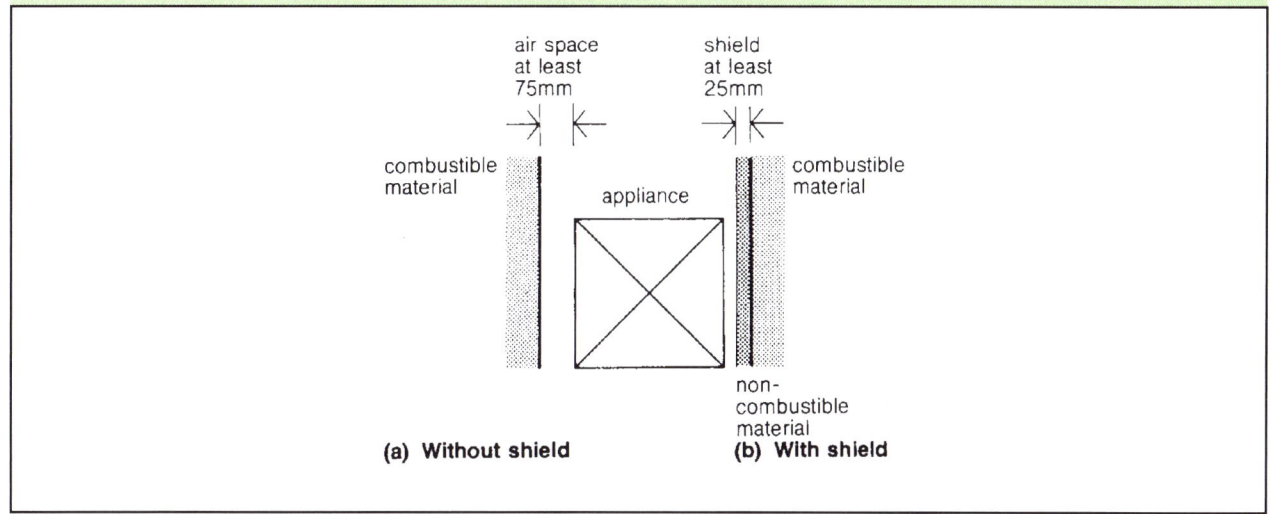

Alternative approach

The requirements may also be met by adopting the relevant recommendations in the publications listed below to achieve an equivalent level of performance to that obtained by following the guidance in this Approved Document:

BS 5440: *Installation and maintenance of flues and ventilation for gas appliances of rated input not exceeding 70kW net (1st, 2nd and 3rd family gases), Part 1: 2000 Specification for installation and maintenance of flues; Part 2: 2000 Specification for installation and maintenance of ventilation for gas appliances.*

BS 5546: *2000 Specification for installation of hot water supplies for domestic purposes, using gas-fired appliances of rated input not exceeding 70kW.*

BS 5864: 1989 *Specification for installation in domestic premises of gas-fired ducted-air heaters of rated input not exceeding 60kW.*

BS 5871: *Specification for installation of gas fires, convector heaters, fire/back boilers and decorative fuel effect gas appliances, Part 1: 2001Gas fires, convector heaters and fire/back boilers and heating stoves (1st, 2nd and 3rd family gases); Part 2: 2001 Inset live fuel effect gas fires of heat input not exceeding 15kW and fire/back boilers (2nd and 3rd family gases); Part 3: 2001 Decorative fuel effect gas appliances of heat input not exceeding 20kW (2nd and 3rd family gases).*

BS 6172: *1990 Specification for installation of domestic gas cooking appliances (1st, 2nd and 3rd family gases).*

BS 6173: 2001 *Specification for installation of gas-fired catering appliances for use in all types of catering establishments (2nd and 3rd family gases).*

BS 6798: *2000 Specification for installation of gas-fired boilers of rated input not exceeding 70kW net.*

Section 4

ADDITIONAL PROVISIONS FOR OIL BURNING APPLIANCES WITH A RATED OUTPUT UP TO 45KW

Note: This section should be read in conjunction with Sections 0 and 1

Scope

4.1 This guidance is relevant to combustion installations designed to burn oils meeting the specifications for Class C2 (Kerosene) and Class D (Gas oil) given in BS 2869:1998 or equivalent.

Appliances fitted in bathrooms and shower rooms

4.2 Open-flued oil-fired appliances should not be installed in rooms such as bathrooms and bedrooms where there is an increased risk of carbon monoxide poisoning. Where locating combustion appliances in such rooms cannot be avoided, a way of meeting the requirements would be to provide room-sealed appliances.

Air supply to appliances

4.3 A way of meeting the requirements would be to adopt the general guidance given in Section 1, starting at Paragraph 1.2 and to provide permanently open air vents as shown in Diagram 4.1 in rooms or spaces containing appliances. An example calculation illustrating the use of this guidance is given in Appendix D. Where manufacturers' installation instructions require greater areas of permanently open air vents than those shown in Diagram 4.1, the manufacturers' advice should be followed.

Size of flues (other than balanced flues and flues designed to discharge through or adjacent to walls)

4.4 Flues should be sized to suit the intended appliance such that they ensure adequate discharge velocity to prevent flow reversal problems but do not impose excessive flow resistances. A way of meeting the requirements would be to use:

a) connecting fluepipes the same size as the appliance flue outlet; and

b) flues in chimneys the same cross sectional area as the appliance flue outlet. When constructing masonry or flueblock chimneys, a way of doing this would be to:

> i) make the flue the same size as the appliance flue outlet; or

> ii) make the flue larger and of a size that would allow the later insertion of a suitable flexible flue liner matching the appliance to be installed.

4.5 Larger flues may need to be provided where appliance manufacturers' installation instructions demand this.

Outlets from flues and flue heights

4.6 The outlet from a flue should be so situated externally as to ensure: the correct operation of a natural draught flue; the intake of air if a balanced flue; and ensure dispersal of the products of combustion.

4.7 A way of meeting the requirement could be to follow the guidance in Diagram 4.2. The separations given in the Table to Diagram 4.2 are minimum values that may have to be increased where there is a risk that local factors such as wind patterns could disrupt the operation of the flue or where a natural draught flue would not be tall enough to clear the products of combustion of an open-flued appliance.

4.8 Flue outlets should be protected with terminal guards if persons could come into contact with them or if they could be damaged. If a flue outlet is in a vulnerable position, such as where the flue discharges at a point within reach of the ground, balcony, veranda or a window, it should be designed to prevent the entry of any matter that could obstruct the flow.

Flues for oil-fired appliances: flue gas temperature

4.9 Satisfactory provision of chimneys and fluepipes depends upon the flue gas temperature to be expected in normal service and separate guidance is given in this Approved Document according to whether the proposed installation will have a flue gas temperature more than or less than 250°C as measured by a suitable method such as those in *OFTEC Standards A 100 or A 101*.

4.10 Flue gas temperatures depend upon appliance types and the age of their design. Older and second hand appliances are likely to produce flue gas temperatures greater than 250°C. Amongst modern appliances, boilers bearing the CE mark, indicating compliance with the Boiler (Efficiency) Regulations (1993), normally have flue gas temperatures not exceeding 250°C. Information for individual appliances should be sought from the manufacturer's installation instructions, from the manufacturers themselves or from OFTEC. Where this is not available, flues should be constructed for an assumed flue gas temperature greater than 250°C.

Diagram 4.1: Free areas of permanently open air vents for oil-fired appliance installations

	Open-flued	Room-sealed
Appliance in a room or space	Open-flued appliance 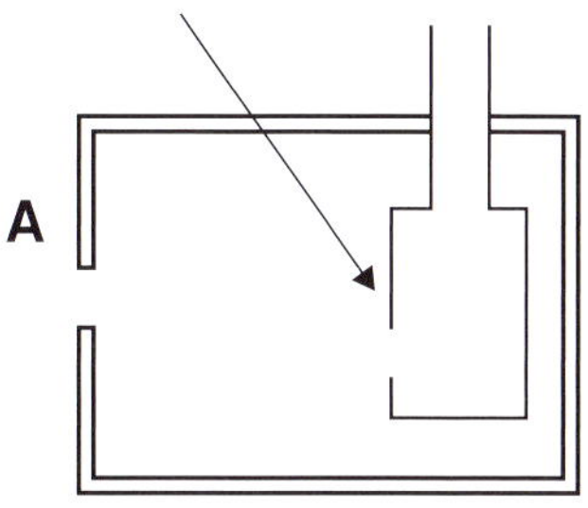 A $A = 550mm^2$ per kW output in excess of 5kW (see Note 3)	Room-sealed appliance 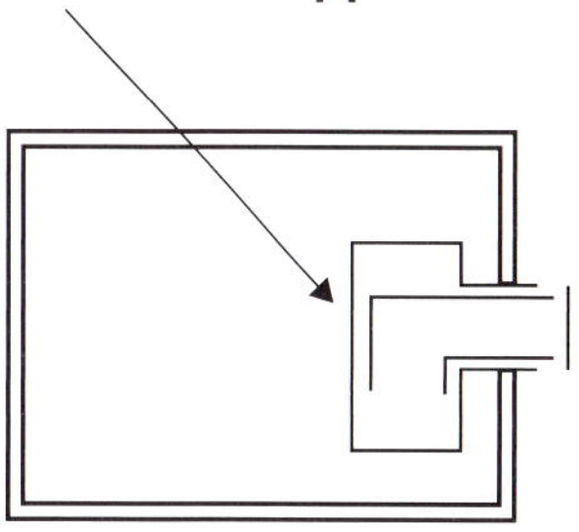 No vent needed
Appliance in an appliance compartment ventilated via an adjoining room or space	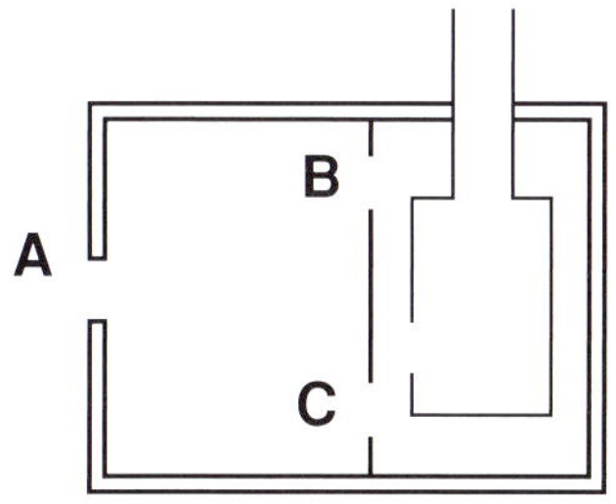 A B C $A = 550mm^2$ per kW output in excess of 5 kW (see Note 3) $B = 1100mm^2$ per kW output $C = 1650mm^2$ per kW output	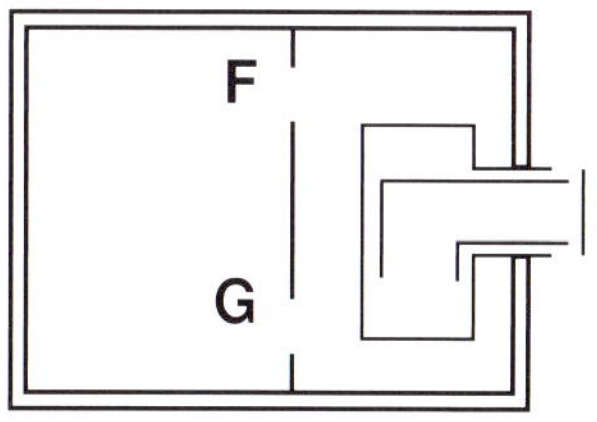 F G $F = 1100mm^2$ per kW output $G = F$
Appliance in an appliance compartment ventilated direct to outside	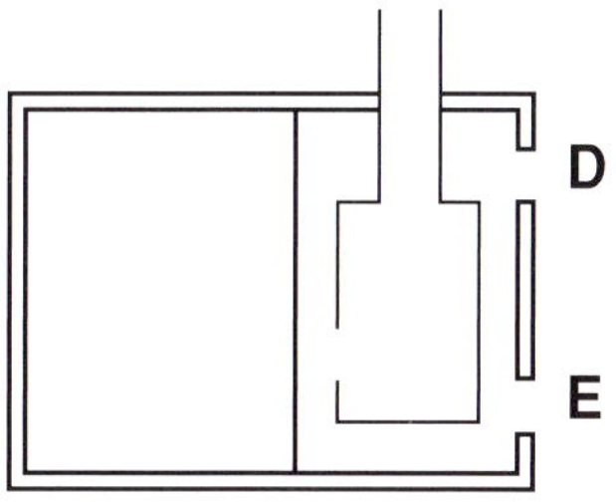 D E $D = 550mm^2$ per kW output $E = 1100mm^2$ per kW output	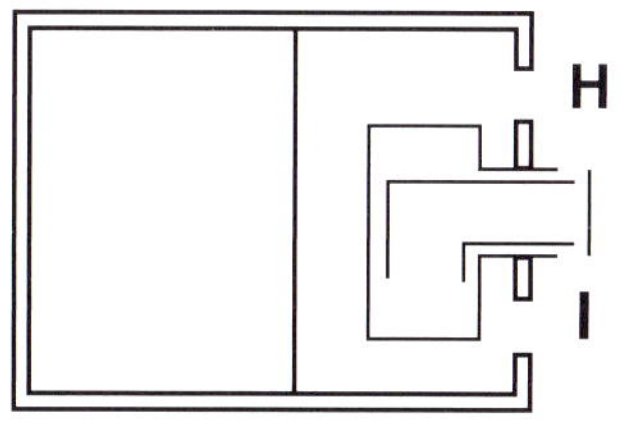 H I $H = 550mm^2$ per kW output $I = H$

Notes:

1. A, D, E, H and I are permanently open vents to the outside. B, C, F and G are permanently open vents between an appliance compartment and a room or space.

2. The area given above is the free area of the vent(s) or the equivalent free area for ventilators of more complex design.

3. Vent A should be increased by a further $550mm^2$ per kW output if the appliance is fitted with a draught break.

4. Divide the area given above in mm^2 by 100 to find the corresponding area in cm^2.

Diagram 4.2: **Location of outlets from flues serving oil-fired appliances**

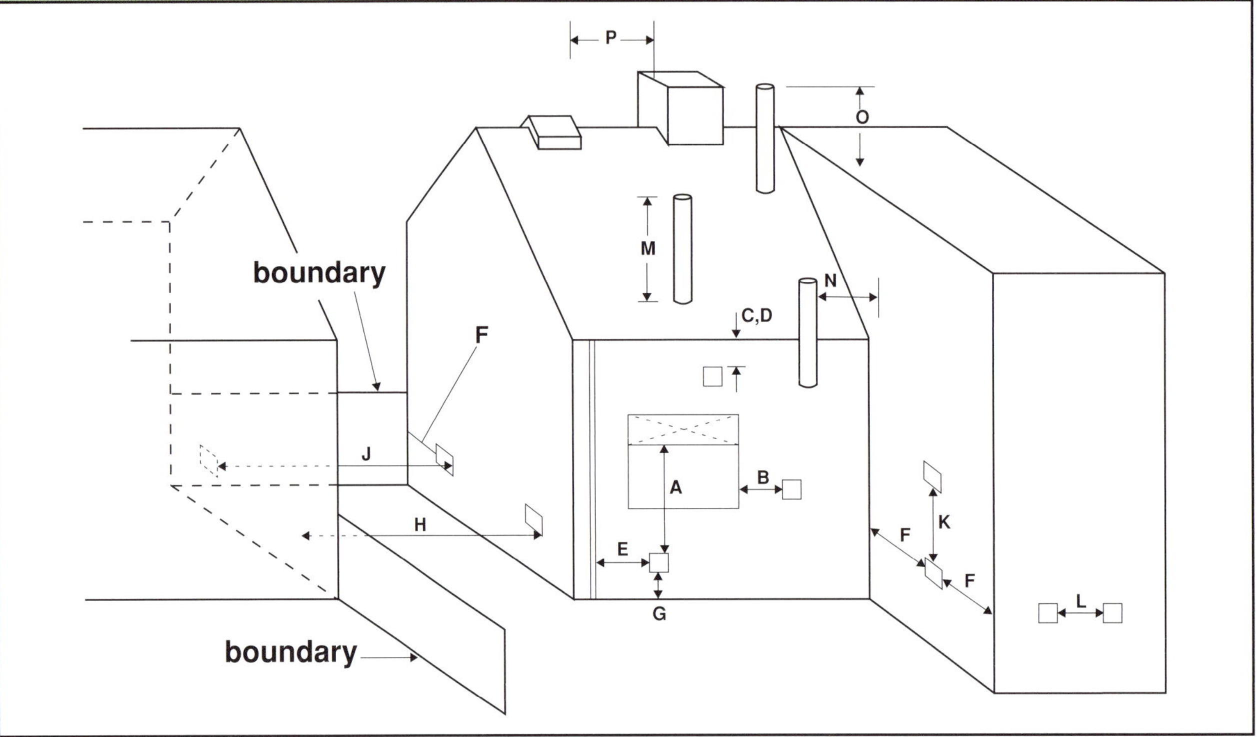

Table to Diagram 4.2: **Location of outlets from flues serving oil-fired appliances**

Minimum separation distances for terminals in mm

Location of outlet (1)		Appliance with pressure jet burner	Appliance with vaporising burner
A	Below an opening (2, 3)	600	should not be used
B	Horizontally to an opening (2, 3)	600	should not be used
C	Below a plastic / painted gutter, drainage pipe or eaves if combustible material protected (4)	75	should not be used
D	Below a balcony or a plastic/painted gutter, drainage pipe or eaves without protection to combustible material	600	should not be used
E	From vertical sanitary pipework	300	should not be used
F	From an external or internal corner or from a surface or boundary alongside the terminal	300	should not be used
G	Above ground or balcony level	300	should not be used
H	From a surface or boundary facing the terminal	600	should not be used
J	From a terminal facing the terminal	1200	should not be used
K	Vertically from a terminal on the same wall	1500	should not be used
L	Horizontally from a terminal on the same wall	750	should not be used
M	Above the highest point of an intersection with the roof	600 (6)	1000 (5)
N	From a vertical structure to the side of the terminal	750 (6)	2300
O	Above a vertical structure which is less than 750mm (pressure jet burner) or 2300mm (vaporising burner) horizontally from the side of the terminal	600 (6)	1000 (5)
P	From a ridge terminal to a vertical structure on the roof	1500	should not be used

Notes:
1. Terminals should only be positioned on walls where appliances have been approved for such configurations when tested in accordance with BS EN 303-1:1999 or OFTEC standards OFS A100 or OFS A101.
2. An opening means an openable element, such as an openable window, or a permanent opening such as a permanently open air vent.
3. Notwithstanding the dimensions above, a terminal should be at least 300mm from combustible material, e.g. a window frame.
4. A way of providing protection of combustible material would be to fit a heat shield at least 750mm wide.
5. Where a terminal is used with a vaporising burner, the terminal should be at least 2300mm horizontally from the roof .
6. Outlets for vertical balanced flues in locations M, N and O should be in accordance with manufacturer's instructions.

Provisions for flue gas temperatures in excess of 250°C

4.11 A way of making satisfactory provision for oil appliances in these cases would be to follow the guidance given in Sections 1 and 2 for connecting fluepipes and masonry or flueblock chimneys or to provide a factory-made metal chimney in accordance with Paragraphs 1.42 to 1.46 in Section 1 (but not Paragraph 1.42(b)). However, other products may be acceptable if they have been independently certified for this purpose.

Provisions for flue gas temperatures not exceeding 250°C

4.12 Satisfactory provision of chimneys and fluepipes for oil appliances in these cases may by achieved by:

a)   following the guidance on the selection of components and the manner of their installation as given in Paragraphs 4.13 to 4.20 below and the references to Section 1;

or (if the intended appliance is new and of known type);

b)   i) using factory-made components that have been independently certified as achieving a performance at least equal to that corresponding to the designation given in Table 4.1 (for the intended appliance type) when tested to an appropriate European chimney standard (BS EN); and

ii) installing these components in accordance with the guidance in Paragraphs 4.13 to 4.20 and Section 1, as relevant, and in accordance with the appliance manufacturer's and component manufacturer's installation instructions.

Connecting fluepipe components

4.13 Connecting fluepipes can be constructed using the following components:

a)   any of the options listed in Paragraph 1.32; or

b)   sheet metal fluepipes as described in BS 715:1993; or

c)   fibre cement pipes as described in BS 7435-1:1991 (1998) or BS 7435-2:1991 (1998); or

d)   any other component that has been independently certified as suitable for this purpose.

Masonry chimneys

4.14 Masonry chimneys can be built in accordance with Paragraphs 1.27 and 1.28 in Section 1.

Flueblock chimneys

4.15 Chimneys can be constructed from factory-made flueblock systems primarily designed for solid fuel, as described in Paragraphs 1.29 and 1.30 in Section 1. They can also be constructed from factory-made flueblock systems comprising straight blocks, recess units, lintel blocks, offset blocks, transfer blocks and jointing materials complying with:

a)   BS 1289-1:1986 for concrete flueblocks; or

b)   BS EN 1806:2000 for clay/ceramic flueblocks, with a performance at least equal to the designation given in Table 4.1 for the intended appliance type.

4.16 Flueblock chimneys should be installed with sealed joints in accordance with the flueblock manufacturer's installation instructions. Where bends or offsets are required, these should be formed using matching factory-made components. Flueblocks which are not intended to be bonded into surrounding masonry should be supported and restrained in accordance with the manufacturer's installation instructions.

Factory-made metal chimneys

4.17 Chimneys for oil-fired appliances can be constructed using the systems described in Paragraphs 1.42 to 1.46 in Section 1.

Location and shielding of flues

4.18 A way of protecting the building fabric from the heat dissipation from flues, where flue gas temperatures are not expected to exceed 250°C, would be to follow the guidance in Table 4.2.

4.19 Where a fluepipe or chimney penetrates a fire compartment wall or floor, it must not breach the fire separation requirements of Part B. See Approved Document B for more guidance.

4.20 Fluepipes and factory-made chimneys should also be guarded if they could be at risk of damage or if they present a hazard to people that is not immediately apparent such as when they traverse intermediate floors out of sight of the appliance.

Relining of flues in chimneys

4.21 Lining or relining flues may be building work and, in any case, such work should be carried out so that the objectives of requirements J2 to J4 are met (see Paragraphs 1.34 and 1.35). For flue liners serving oil appliances, ways of meeting the requirements include the use of:

a) linings suitable for use if the flue gas temperature can be expected to exceed 250°C such as:

    i) liners as described in Paragraph 1.27;

    ii) liners as described in Paragraph 2.20;

    iii) flexible stainless steel liners independently certified as complying with BS 715:1993;

    iv) other systems which have been independently certified as suitable for this purpose;

b) linings suitable for use if the flue gas temperature is unlikely to exceed 250°C such as:

    i) any of the linings described in (a) above;

    ii) other systems which have been independently certified as suitable for this purpose;

    iii) (if the appliance is new and of known type) flue lining systems that have been independently certified as having a performance at least equal to that corresponding to the designation given in Table 4.1 for the intended appliance type.

4.22 Flexible metal flue liners should be installed in one complete length without joints within the chimney. Other than for sealing at the top and the bottom, the space between the chimney and the liner should be left empty unless this is contrary to the manufacturer's instructions. Double skin flexible flue liners should be installed in accordance with manufacturer's installation instructions. BS 715:1993 liners should be installed in accordance with BS 5440-1:2000.

Flues for appliances burning Class D oil

4.23 Flues which may be expected to serve appliances burning Class D oil should be made of materials which are resistant to acids of sulphur.

Hearths for oil fired appliances

4.24 Hearths are needed to prevent the building catching fire and, whilst it is not a health and safety provision, it is customary to top them with a tray for collecting spilled fuel.

Table 4.1: Minimum performance designations for chimney and fluepipe components for use with new oil-fired appliances with flue gas temperature less than 250°C

Appliance type	Minimum designation (See Notes)	
Boiler – pressure jet (including combination) Boiler – condensing Cooker – pressure jet	T160 P2 O D 1 T160 P2 O D 2	Class C2 oil Class D oil
Cooker – vaporising burner Room heater - vaporising burner	T160 N2 O D 1 T160 N2 O D 2	Class C2 oil Class D oil

Notes:

1. The designation of chimney products is described in Paragraph 0.4(9). The BS EN for the product will specify its full designation and marking requirements.

2. These are default designations. Where appliance manufacturer's installation instructions specify a higher designation, this should be complied with.

Table 4.2 : Protecting buildings from hot flues for flue gas temperatures not more than 250ºC

Flue within:	Protection measures
Connecting fluepipe Factory-made chimney complying with BS 715:1993	Flues should be at least 25mm from any combustible material (measured from the outer surface of the flue wall, or the outer surface of the inner wall in the case of multi-walled products). Where passing through a combustible wall, floor or roof (other than a compartment wall floor or roof) this separation can be achieved by a non-combustible sleeve enclosing the fluepipe or chimney with a 25mm airspace to the relevant flue wall. (The airspace could be wholly or partially filled with non-combustible insulating material.)
Factory-made chimney complying with BS 4543-1:1990 (1996),* BS 4543-2:1990 (1996), BS 4543-3:1990 (1996)	Install in accordance with Paragraph 1.45 of this Approved Document.
Masonry chimney	Provide at least 25mm of masonry between flues and any combustible material.
Flueblock chimney	Provide flueblock walls at least 25mm thick.
Flue assemblies for room-sealed appliances	a) flues passing through combustible walls should be surrounded by insulating material at least 50mm thick b) provide a clearance of at least 50mm from the edge of the flue outlet to any combustible wall cladding.

* BS 4543-1:1990 (1996) withdrawn April 2000; partially superseded by BS EN 1859:2000

4.25 If the operation of an appliance is unlikely to cause the temperature of the floor below it to exceed 100°C, as shown using an appropriate test procedure such as those in *OFTEC Standards A 100 and A 101*, special measures may be unnecessary beyond the provision of a rigid, imperforate, and non-absorbent sheet of non-combustible material such as a steel tray. This may be provided as an integral part of the appliance.

4.26 If the appliance could cause the temperature of the floor below it to exceed 100°C, a more substantial hearth is required. A way of meeting the requirement would be to provide a hearth of solid non-combustible material at least 125mm thick (which may include the thickness of any non-combustible floor) with plan dimensions not less than those shown in Diagram 2.8 in Section 2. It should have no combustible material below it unless there is an air space of at least 50mm between the material and the underside of the hearth, or there is a distance of at least 250mm between the material and the top of the hearth (see Diagram 2.9 in Section 2).

4.27 To provide a region around the appliance which is free of any combustible material, the appliance should not be placed closer to the edges of the hearth nor closer to any combustible material which is laid over the hearth than the distances shown in Diagram 4.3. The perimeter of this safe region should be marked to provide a warning to the building occupants and to discourage combustible floor finishes such as carpet from being laid too close to the appliance. A way of achieving this would be to provide a change in level.

Shielding of oil fired appliances

4.28 Combustible materials adjacent to oil fired appliances may need protection from the effects of heat. Special measures may be unnecessary if the materials will not be subjected to temperatures in excess of 100°C but otherwise a way of meeting the requirement would be to protect combustible fabric with:

a)   a shield of non-combustible material, such as insulating board with fire resistant surface; or

b)   an air space of at least 75mm (see Diagram 3.9 in Section 3).

4.29 Appliances independently certified as having surface temperatures during normal operation of no more than 100°C would not normally require shielding.

Alternative approach

The requirements may also be met by adopting the relevant recommendations in the publication listed below to achieve an equivalent level of performance to that obtained by following the guidance in this Approved Document:

BS 5410: *Code of practice for oil firing*, Part 1: 1997 *Installations up to 45kW output capacity for space heating and hot water supply purposes.*

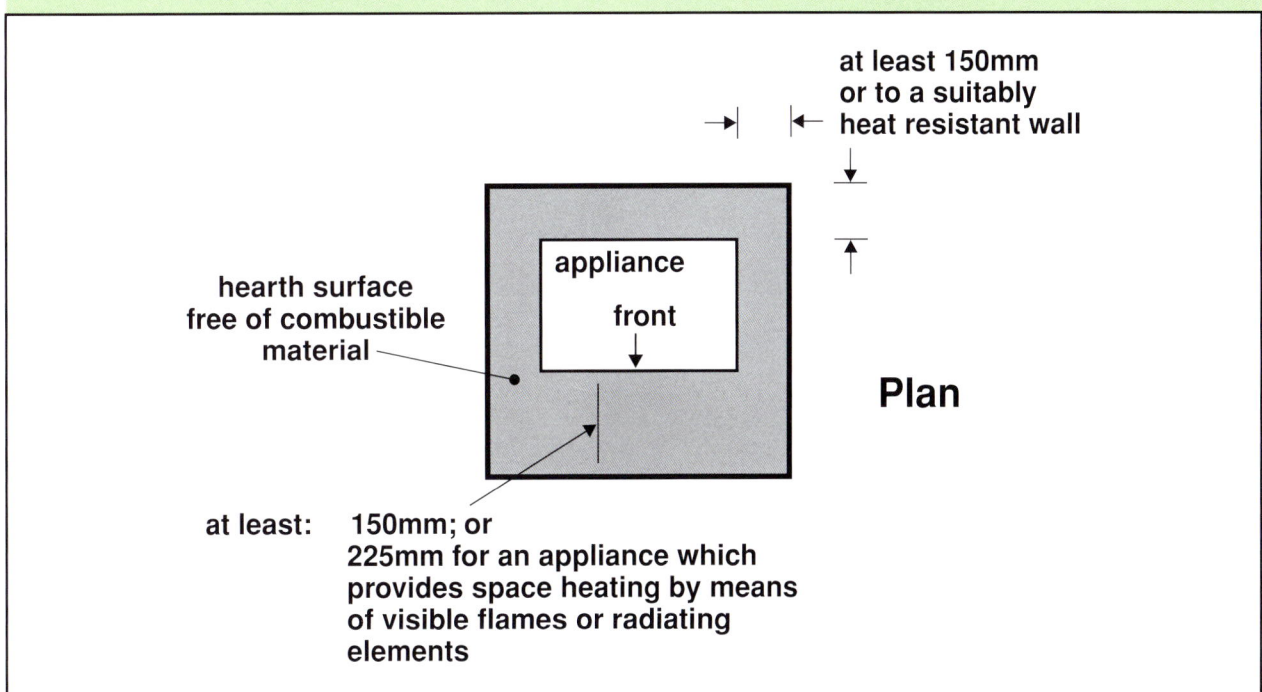

Diagram 4.3: **Location of an oil-fired appliance in relation to its hearth. Minimum dimensions of the heat resistant material in the hearth and the clear zone of non-combustible surface**

at least 150mm or to a suitably heat resistant wall

appliance front

hearth surface free of combustible material

Plan

at least: 150mm; or 225mm for an appliance which provides space heating by means of visible flames or radiating elements

Section 5

PROVISIONS FOR LIQUID FUEL STORAGE AND SUPPLY

Performance

5.1   In the Secretary of State's view requirements J5 and J6 will be met if:

a)   oil and LPG fuel storage installations including the pipework connecting them to the combustion appliances in the buildings they serve are located and constructed so that they are reasonably protected from fires which may occur in buildings or beyond boundaries;

b)   oil storage tanks, their ancillary equipment and the pipework connecting them to combustion appliances in buildings used wholly or mainly for private dwellings:

- i)   are reasonably resistant to physical damage and corrosion and are designed and installed so as to minimise the risk of oil escaping during the filling or maintenance of the tank; and

- ii)   incorporate secondary containment when there is a significant risk of pollution; and

- iii)   are labelled with information on how to respond to a leak.

Heating oil storage installations

5.2   Guidance is given in this Approved Document on ways of meeting requirements J5 and J6 when proposing to construct oil storage systems with above-ground or semi-buried tanks of 3500 litres capacity or less, used exclusively for heating oil. Heating oils comprise Class C2 oil (kerosene) or Class D oil (gas oil) as specified in BS 2869:1998. A way of meeting requirements J5 and J6 for such installations would be to follow the relevant recommendations in BS 5410-1:1997, whilst also adopting the guidance in paragraphs 5.4 to 5.12 below.

5.3   Requirement J6 does not apply to oil storage systems where the capacity of the tank exceeds 3500 litres, or where the tank is fully buried or where the building served is not wholly or mainly used as one or more private dwellings. However requirement J5 applies to oil storage systems serving buildings of all descriptions, where the capacity of the tank exceeds 90 litres, with no upper capacity limit on application, and including cases where the tank is buried. For tanks with capacities in excess of 3500 litres, advice on ways of complying with requirements J5 and any other fire precautions legislation, may be sought from the Fire Authority. In England tanks serving buildings which are not wholly or mainly used as private dwellings are likely to be subject to the Control of Pollution (Oil Storage) (England) Regulations 2001 (see paragraph 5.7 below).

Protective measures against fire

5.4   A way of achieving compliance with requirement J5 would be to adopt the guidance given in Table 5.1 which also offers advice on reducing the risk of fuel storage system fires igniting buildings and to make provision against the installation becoming overgrown. This can be achieved with a hard surface beneath the tank such as concrete, or paving slabs at least 42mm thick, extending out at least 300mm beyond the perimeter of the tank (or its external skin if it is of the integrally bunded type).

5.5   Fire walls should be built to be stable so as not to pose a danger to people around them. A way of achieving this when constructing masonry walls would be to follow the guidance on wall thickness in relation to height given in *Your garden walls Better to be safe than sorry* (see Page 68).

Table 5.1 : **Fire protection for oil storage tanks**	
Location of tank	Protection usually satisfactory
Within a building.	Locate tanks in a place of special fire hazard which should be directly ventilated to outside. Without prejudice to the need for compliance with all the requirements in Schedule 1, the need to comply with Part B should particularly be taken into account.
Less than 1800mm from any part of a building	a) Make building walls imperforate (1) within 1800mm of tanks with at least 30 minutes fire resistance (2) to internal fire and construct eaves within 1800mm of tanks and extending 300mm beyond each side of tanks with at least 30 minutes fire resistance to external fire and with non-combustible cladding; or b) Provide a fire wall (3) between the tank and any part of the building within 1800mm of the tank and construct eaves as in (a) above. The fire wall should extend at least 300mm higher and wider than the affected parts of the tank.
Less than 760mm from a boundary	Provide a fire wall between the tank and the boundary or a boundary wall having at least 30 minutes fire resistance to fire on either side. The fire wall or the boundary wall should extend at least 300mm higher and wider than the top and sides of the tank.
At least 1800mm from the building and at least 760mm from a boundary	No further provisions necessary

Notes:

1. Excluding small openings such as air bricks etc.

2. Fire resistance in terms of insulation, integrity and stability.

3. Fire walls are imperforate non-combustible walls or screens, such as masonry walls or steel screens.

Oil supply pipe systems: means of automatic isolation

5.6 A way of meeting the requirement would be to install fuel pipework which is resistant to the effects of fire and to fit a proprietary fire valve system in accordance with the relevant recommendations in BS 5410-1:1997, Sections 8.2 and 8.3.

Provisions where there is a risk of oil pollution

5.7 The Control of Pollution (Oil Storage) (England) Regulations 2001 (SI 2001/2954) come into force on 1 March 2002. They apply to a wide range of oil storage installations in England, but they do not apply to the storage of oil on any premises used wholly or mainly as one or more private dwellings, if the capacity of the tank is 3500 litres or less.

5.8 Requirement J6 applies to oil storage tanks of 3500 litres or less serving combustion appliances in buildings used wholly or mainly as private dwellings. In such cases, secondry containment should be provided where there is a significant risk of oil pollution. For the purposes of requirement J6, there is a significant risk of pollution if the oil storage installation:

a)   has a total capacity of more than 2500 litres; or

b)   is located within 10m of inland freshwaters or coastal waters; or

c)   is located where spillage could run into an open drain or to a loose fitting manhole cover; or

d)   is located within 50m of sources of potable water, such as a wells, bore-holes or springs; or

e)   is located where oil spilled from the installation could reach the waters listed above by running across hard ground; or

f)   is located where tank vent pipe outlets cannot be seen from the intended filling point.

5.9 Inland freshwaters include streams, rivers reservoirs and lakes, as well as ditches and ground drainage (including perforated drainage pipes) that feed into them.

5.10 When secondary containment is considered necessary, a way of meeting the requirement would be to:

a)   provide an integrally bunded prefabricated tank; or

b)   construct a bund from masonry or concrete in accordance with the general guidance in *Above Ground Oil Storage Tanks: PPG2* and the specific advice in *Masonry Bunds for Oil Storage Tanks* or *Concrete Bunds for Oil Storage Tanks*, as appropriate (see Page 68). However:

i)   where the bund walls are part of the walls of a chamber or building enclosing the tank, any door through such walls should be above bund level; and

ii)   specialist advice should be sought where the bund has a structural role as part of a building.

5.11 Bunds, whether part of prefabricated tank systems or constructed on site, should have a capacity of at least 110% of the largest tank they contain.

5.12 An oil storage installation should carry a label in a prominent position giving advice on what to do if an oil spill occurs and the telephone number of the Environment Agency's Emergency Hotline (see Page 66).

LPG storage installations

5.13 LPG installations are controlled by legislation enforced by the HSE or their agents. Factors which determine the amount of building work necessary for a LPG storage installation to comply include its capacity, whether or not tanks are installed above or below ground and the nature of the premises they serve. A storage installation may be shown to comply with the legislation by constructing it in accordance with an appropriate industry Code of Practice, prepared in consultation with the HSE. However, for an installation of up to 1.1 tonne capacity, whose tank stands in the open air, following the guidance in this Approved Document and the relevant guidance in Approved Document B, will normally ensure that no further building work is needed to comply with other legislation.

Tank location and protective measures

5.14 For LPG storage systems of up to 1.1 tonne capacity, comprising one tank standing in the open air, a way of meeting the requirement J5 would be to comply with the relevant recommendations in the LP Gas Association CODE OF PRACTICE 1 *Bulk LPG Storage at Fixed Installations Part 1* (see Page 66 and 68) whilst also adopting the following guidance:

5.15 The LPG tank should be installed outdoors and not within an open pit. The tank should be adequately separated from buildings, the boundary (see Paragraph 0.4(4)) and any fixed sources of ignition to enable safe dispersal in the event of venting or leaks and in the event of fire to reduce the risk of fire spreading. A way of meeting the requirements in normal situations would be to adopt the separation distances in Table 5.2 and Diagram 5.1 which also offers advice on reducing the risk of LPG storage fires igniting the building. Drains, gullies and cellar hatches within the separation distances should be protected from gas entry.

Diagram 5.1: **Separation or shielding of liquefied petroleum gas tanks of up to 1.1 tonne capacity from buildings, boundaries and fixed sources of ignition**

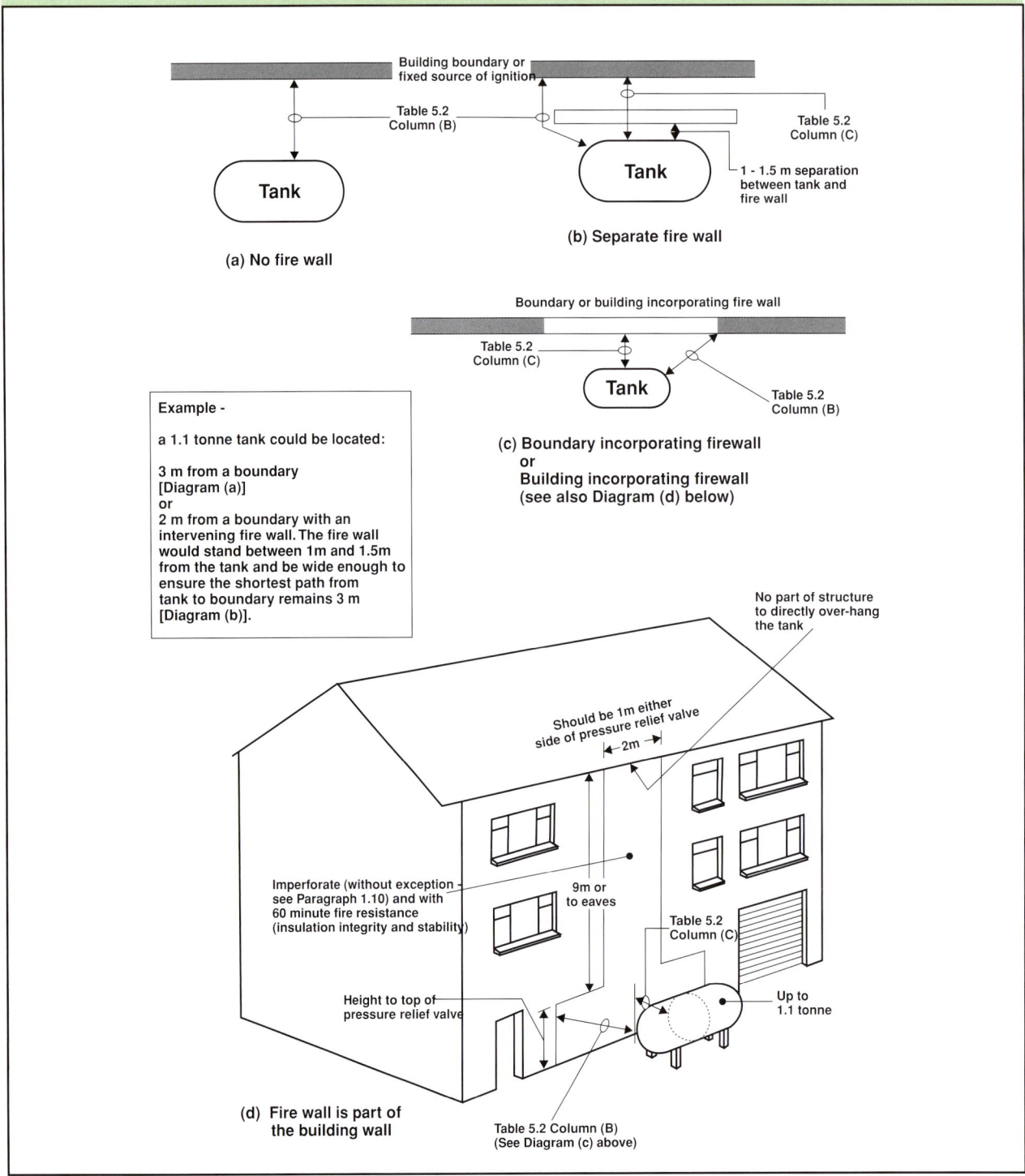

(a) No fire wall

(b) Separate fire wall

(c) Boundary incorporating firewall
or
Building incorporating firewall
(see also Diagram (d) below)

Example -

a 1.1 tonne tank could be located:

3 m from a boundary
[Diagram (a)]
or
2 m from a boundary with an intervening fire wall. The fire wall would stand between 1m and 1.5m from the tank and be wide enough to ensure the shortest path from tank to boundary remains 3 m [Diagram (b)].

(d) Fire wall is part of the building wall

5.16 Fire walls may be free-standing walls built between the tank and the building, boundary and fixed source of ignition (see Diagram 5.1(b)) or a part of the building or a boundary wall belonging to the property. Where a fire wall is part of the building or a boundary wall, it should be located in accordance with Diagram 5.1(c) and, if part of the building, constructed in accordance with Diagram 5.1(d).

5.17 Suitable fire walls would be imperforate and of solid masonry, concrete or similar construction. They should have a fire

resistance (insulation, integrity and stability) of at least 30 minutes but, if part of the building as shown in Diagram 5.1(d), they should have a fire resistance (insulation, integrity and stability) of at least 60 minutes. To ensure good ventilation, fire walls should not normally be built on more than one side of a tank.

5.18 A fire wall should be at least as high as the pressure relief valve. It should extend horizontally such that the separation specified in Table 5.2 (Column B) is maintained:

a)   when measured around the ends of the fire wall as shown in Diagram 5.1(b); or

b)   when measured to the ends of the fire wall as shown in Diagram 5.1(c), if the fire wall is the boundary or part of the building.

Location and support of cylinders

5.19 Where an LPG storage installation consists of a set of cylinders, a way of meeting the requirements would be to follow the provisions below and as shown in Diagram 5.2.

5.20 Provisions should enable cylinders to stand upright, secured by straps or chains against a wall outside the building in a well ventilated position at ground level, where they

are readily accessible, reasonably protected from physical damage and where they do not obstruct exit routes from the building. Satisfactory building work provisions would be to provide a firm level base such as concrete at least 50mm thick or paving slabs bedded on mortar at a location so that cylinder valves will be:

a)   at least 1m horizontally and 300mm vertically from openings in the building or heat sources such as flue terminals and tumble-dryer vents; and

b)   at least 2m horizontally from drains without traps, unsealed gullies or cellar hatches unless an intervening wall not less than 250mm high is provided.

Table 5.2 : Fire protection for LPG storage tanks (see Diagram 5.1)

(A) Capacity of tank not exceeding (tonnes):	Minimum separation distances from buildings, boundaries or fixed sources of ignition (metres)	
	(B) To a tank with no fire wall or to a tank around a fire wall	(C) To a tank shielded by a fire wall
0.25	2.5	0.3
1.1	3	1.5

Diagram 5.2 : Location of LPG cylinders

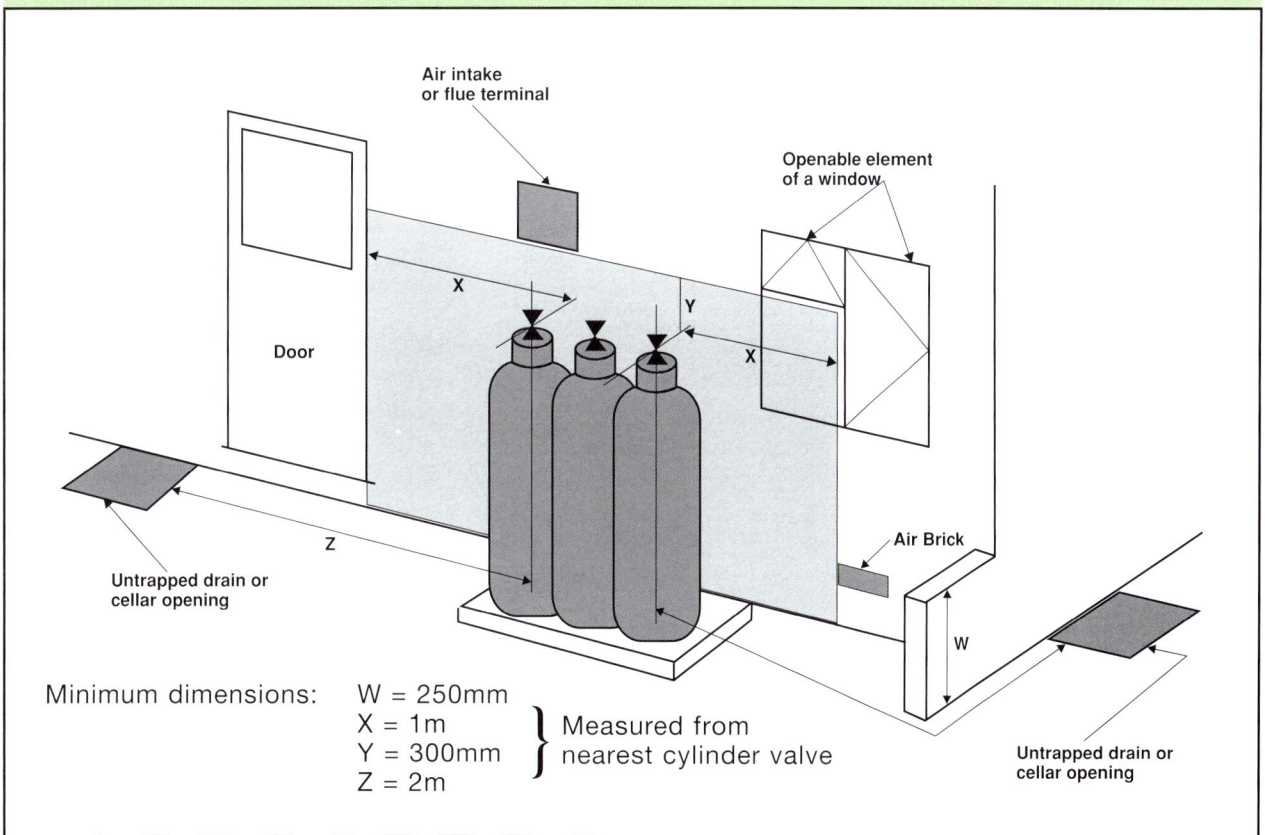

Minimum dimensions: W = 250mm, X = 1m, Y = 300mm, Z = 2m } Measured from nearest cylinder valve

Appendix A

CHECKLIST FOR CHECKING AND TESTING OF HEARTHS, FIREPLACES, FLUES AND CHIMNEYS (SEE PARAGRAPH 1.53): EXAMPLES

Hearths, Fireplaces, flues and chimneys

This checklist can help you to ensure hearths, fireplaces, flues and chimneys are satisfactory. If you have been directly engaged, copies should also be offered to the client and to the Building Control Body to show what you have done to comply with the requirements of Part J. If you are a sub-contractor, a copy should be offered to the main contractor.

1. **Building address, where work has been carried out** ....

....

....

		Example:	Example:	Example:
2.	**Identification of hearth, fireplace, chimney or flue.**	Fireplace in lounge	Gas fire in rear addition bedroom	Small boiler room
3.	**Firing capability: solid fuel/gas/oil/all.**	All	Gas only	Oil only
4.	**Intended type of appliance.** **State type or make. If open fire give finished fireplace opening dimensions.**	Open fire 480 W x 560 H (mm)	Radiant/convector fire 6kW input	Oil fired boiler 18kW output {pressure jet}
5.	**Ventilation provisions for the appliance:** **State type and area of permanently open air vents.**	2 through wall ventilators each 10,000mm^2 (100cm^2)	Not fitted	Vents to outside: Top 9,900mm^2 Bottom 19,800mm^2
6.	**Chimney or flue construction**			
a)	**State the type or make and whether new or existing.**	New. Brick with clay liners	Existing masonry	S.S. prefab to BS4543-2
b)	**Internal flue size (and equivalent height, where calculated - natural draught gas appliances only).**	200mm Ø	125mm Ø (H_e=3.3m)	127mm Ø
c)	**If clay or concrete flue liners used confirm they are correctly jointed with socket end uppermost and state jointing materials used.**	Sockets uppermost Jointed by fire cement	Not applicable	Not applicable
d)	**If an existing chimney has been refurbished with a new liner, type or make of liner fitted.**	Not applicable to BS 715	Flexible metal liner	Not applicable
e)	**Details of flue outlet terminal and diagram reference.**			
	Outlet Detail:	Smith Ltd Louvred pot 200mm Ø	125mm Ø GC1 terminal	Maker's recomm-ended terminal
	Complies with:	As Diagram 2.2 AD J	As BS 5440-1: 2000 Figure C.1	As Diagram 4.2 AD J
f)	**Number and angle of bends.**	2 x 45°	2 x 45°	1 x 90° Tee
g)	**provision for cleaning and recommended frequency.**	Sweep annually via fireplace opening	Annual service by CORGI engineer	Sweep annually via base of Tee and via appliance
7.	**Hearth. Form of construction. New or existing?**	New. Tiles on concrete floor. 125mm thick. As Diagram 2.9 AD J	Existing hearth for solid fuel fire, with fender.	New. Solid floor Min 125mm concrete above DPM. As Diagram 4.3 AD J
8	**Inspection and testing after completion** **Tests carried out by:** **Tests (Appx E in AD J 2002 ed) and results**	Inspected and tested by J Smith, Smith Building Co	Tested by J Smith, CORGI Reg no. 12345	Tested by J Smith, The Oil Heating Co.
Flue inspection	visual	Not possible, bends	Not possible, bends	Checked to Section 10, BS7566:Part 3:
	sweeping	OK	Not applicable	1992 – OK
	coring ball	OK	Not applicable	
	smoke	OK	Not applicable	OK
	Appliance (where included) spillage	Not included	OK	OK

I/We the undersigned confirm that the above details are correct. In my opinion, these works comply with the relevant requirements in Part J of Schedule 1 to the Building Regulations.

Print name and title ....Profession ....

Capacity ... (e.g. "Proprietor of Smith's Flues", Authorising Engineer for Brown plc) ....Tel no ....

Address ....Postcode.........…….........

Signed ....Date ....

Registered membership of ... (e.g. CORGI, OFTEC, HETAS, NACE, NACS) ....

This page may be copied to provide certificates for use. (Use one certificate for each hearth, fireplace, flue or chimney)

CHECKLIST

Hearths, Fireplaces, flues and chimneys

This checklist can help you to ensure hearths, fireplaces, flues and chimneys are satisfactory. If you have been directly engaged, copies should also be offered to the client and to the Building Control Body to show what you have done to comply with the requirements of Part J. If you are a sub-contractor, a copy should be offered to the main contractor.

1. **Building address, where work has been carried out** ....
....
....

2. **Identification of hearth, fireplace, chimney or flue.**

3. **Firing capability: solid fuel/gas/oil/all.**

4. **Intended type of appliance.**
   State type or make. If open fire give finished fireplace opening dimensions.

5. **Ventilation provisions for the appliance:**
   State type and area of permanently open air vents.

6. **Chimney or flue construction**

a) **State the type or make and whether new or existing.**

b) **Internal flue size (and equivalent height, where calculated - natural draught gas appliances only).**

c) **If clay or concrete flue liners used confirm they are correctly jointed with socket end uppermost and state jointing materials used.**

d) **If an existing chimney has been refurbished with a new liner, type or make of liner fitted.**

e) **Details of flue outlet terminal and diagram reference.**
   Outlet Detail:

   Complies with:

f) **Number and angle of bends.**

g) **provision for cleaning and recommended frequency.**

7. **Hearth. Form of construction. New or existing?**

8 **Inspection and testing after completion**
   Tests carried out by:
   Tests (Appx E in AD J 2002 ed) and results
   Flue   **visual**
   inspection   **sweeping**
                          coring ball
                           smoke
   Appliance (where included) spillage

I/We the undersigned confirm that the above details are correct. In my opinion, these works comply with the relevant requirements in Part J of Schedule 1 to the Building Regulations.

Print name and title ....Profession ....

Capacity ....Tel no ....

Address ....Postcode......................

Signed ....Date ....

Registered membership of ... (e.g. CORGI, OFTEC, HETAS, NACE, NACS) ....

Appendix B

OPENING AREAS OF LARGE OR UNUSUAL FIREPLACES (SEE PARAGRAPH 2.7)

B1 The opening area of a fireplace should be calculated from the following formula:

$$\text{Fireplace opening area (mm}^2) = \left(\begin{array}{c} \text{Total horizontal length} \\ \text{of fireplace opening} \\ \text{L (mm)} \end{array} \right) \times \left(\begin{array}{c} \text{Height of fireplace} \\ \text{opening} \\ \text{H (mm)} \end{array} \right)$$

B2 Examples of L and H for large and unusual fireplace openings are shown in Diagram B1.

Diagram B1: **Large or unusual fireplace openings. (Note: for use with this Appendix, measure L, H and W in mm)**

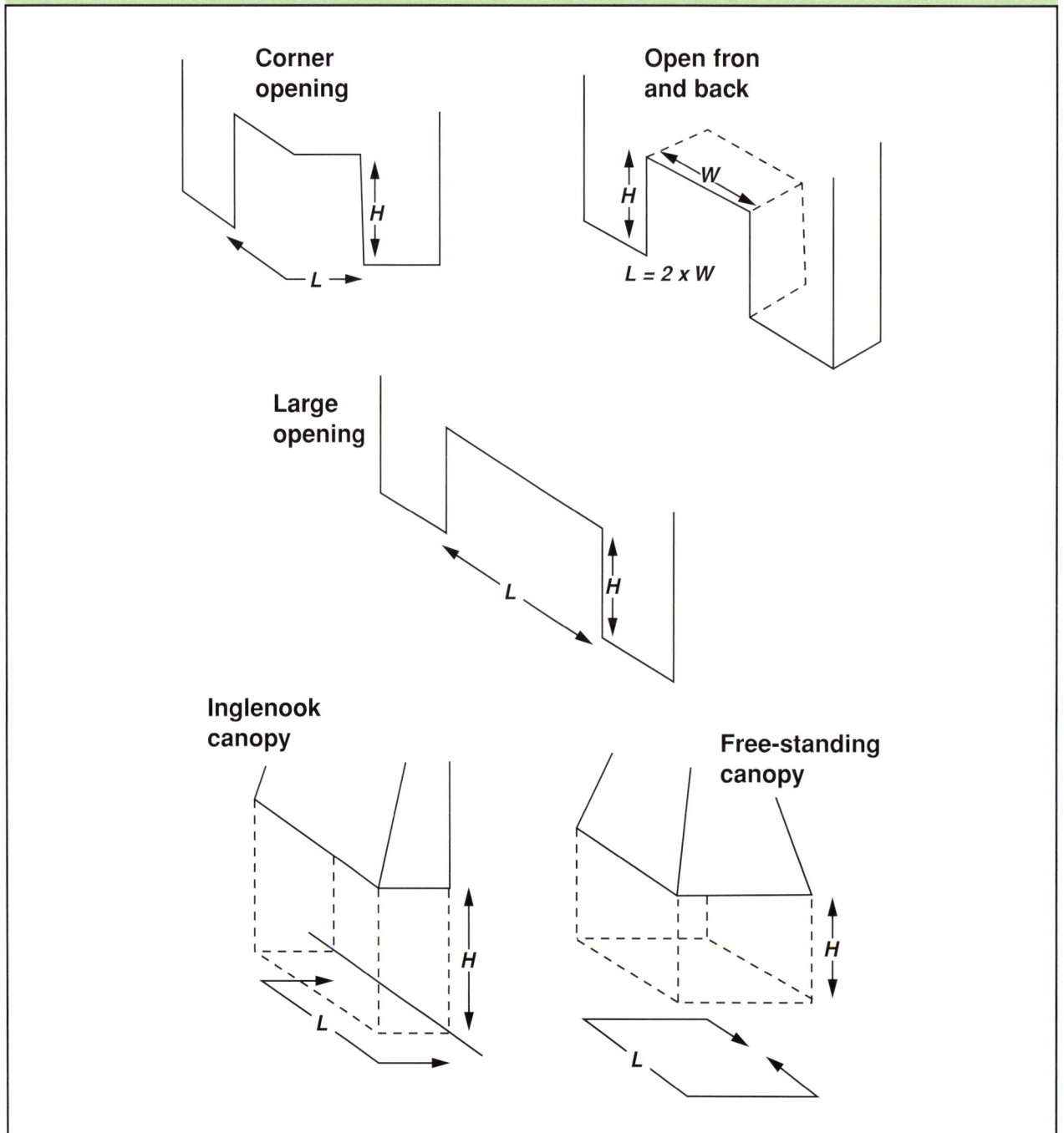

Appendix C

EXAMPLE CALCULATION OF THE VENTILATION REQUIREMENTS OF A GAS-FIRED APPLIANCE (SEE DIAGRAM 3.2)

C1   An open-flued boiler with a rated input of 15kW (net) is installed in an appliance compartment such as a boiler room, which is ventilated directly to the outside. The design of the boiler is such that it requires cooling air in these circumstances.

C2   The cooling air is exhausted via vent D, which has an area:

$$15kW \times 500 \; \frac{mm^2}{kW} = 7\;500mm^2$$

C3   Vent E allows the cooling air to enter, as well as admitting the air needed for combustion and the safe operation of the flue. It has an area:

$$15kW \times 1000 \; \frac{mm^2}{kW} = 15\;000mm^2$$

C4   The ventilation areas in cm^2 can be found by dividing the results given above in mm^2 by 100.

Appendix D

EXAMPLE CALCULATION OF THE VENTILATION REQUIREMENTS OF AN OIL-FIRED APPLIANCE (SEE DIAGRAM 4.1)

D1 An open-flued appliance is installed in an appliance compartment such as a cupboard, which is ventilated via an adjoining room. The appliance has a rated output of 11kW, i.e. 6kW more than the rating at which permanent ventilation openings become necessary for the adjoining room.

D2 Air for combustion and the safe operation of the flue enters the adjoining room partially through infiltration, with the balance entering via vent A, whose area is calculated as follows:

$$(11kW - 5kW) \times 550 \; \frac{mm^2}{kW} = 3\,300mm^2$$

D3 The cooling air for the appliance compartment is exhausted through vent B which has an area:

$$11kW \times 1100 \; \frac{mm^2}{kW} = 12\,100mm^2$$

D4 All of the air for combustion and the safe operation of the flue as well as cooling air enters the appliance compartment through vent C which has an area:

$$11kW \times 1650 \; \frac{mm^2}{kW} = 18\,150mm^2$$

D5 The ventilation areas in cm² can be found by dividing the results given above in mm² by 100.

Appendix E

METHODS OF CHECKING COMPLIANCE WITH REQUIREMENT J2. (SEE PARAGRAPH 1.36 AND 1.53)

E1   This Appendix describes ways of checking the compliance with J2 of existing, relined or new flues, and (where included in the work) the combustion appliance. It only applies to natural draught flues intended for open-flued appliances. The procedures described are only used to assess whether the flue in the chimney, the connecting fluepipe (and flue gas passages in the appliance) are free of obstruction and acceptably gastight. In addition, appliance performance tests, including flue spillage tests to check for compliance with J2, should be carried out when an appliance is commissioned to check for compliance with Part L and as required by the Gas Safety (Installation and Use) Regulations.

E2   Tests on flues should be carried out at the most appropriate time during the building work. Where possible, for example, smoke tests should be performed when the structure of a chimney is visible and before the application of finishes such as plaster or dry lining that could obscure sight of smoke leakage during testing.

Testing applications

Tests for existing flues

E3   Flues in existing chimneys can be obstructed by nests, debris resulting from deterioration of the structure (e.g. brickwork, flue lining material or pieces of chimney pot) and by soot and tar. Flues in existing chimneys may also leak as a result of holes or cracks appearing in the structure and linings, particularly at joints. The top, exposed part of a chimney is particularly prone to decay. A way of checking the state of a flue prior to bringing it back into use would be to do the following:

a)   Sweep the flue. This is intended to clean the flue to demonstrate that it is essentially free from obstructions and to enable better visual inspection and testing of the flue. Tar deposits caused by burning wood may be especially hard to dislodge and should be removed. The debris that comes down the chimney when sweeping should be examined for excessive quantities of lining or brick that are signs that further repairs are necessary;

b)   Carry out a visual inspection of the accessible parts to identify:

    i)   Deterioration in the structure, connections or linings which could

affect the flue's gastightness and safe performance with the proposed combustion appliance. Examine the interior of the flue and the exterior of the chimney including in the roof space. The presence of smoke or tar stains on the exterior of a chimney/breast are signs of leaks that possibly indicate damage;

    ii)   Modifications made whilst the flue was out of service, such as the fitting of a ventilator terminal, which would be incompatible with using the flue with the intended appliance;

    iii)   Correct lining and lining sizes for the proposed new application;

c)   Perform checks where necessary to demonstrate that the flue is free from restriction: a visual check may be sufficient where the full length of the flue can be seen. In cases of doubt, a way of checking this would be to carry out a coring ball test;

d)   Check the operation and gastightness of the flue by carrying out a smoke test.

New masonry and flueblock chimneys

E4   Check during construction that liners are installed the right way up, with sockets facing upwards and joints are sealed so that moisture and condensate will be contained in the chimney.

E5   Flues in new masonry chimneys can be obstructed, particularly at bends, by debris left during construction or by excess mortar falling into the flue or by jointing material extruded from between liners and flueblocks. The flues should be checked to demonstrate that they have been correctly constructed and are free of restrictions and acceptably gas-tight.

A way of checking the condition of a new flue prior to bringing it into use would be to do the following:

a)   A visual inspection of the accessible parts to check that the lining, liners or flueblocks are of the correct materials and of suitable size for the proposed application;

b)   Perform checks where necessary to demonstrate that the flue is free from restriction: a visual check may be sufficient where the full length of the flue can be seen. In cases of doubt, a way of checking this would be to carry out a coring ball test or to sweep the flue, which may be more effective at removing flexible debris that might not be dislodged by a coring ball;

c)   Check the operation and gas-tightness of the flue by carrying out a smoke test.

New factory made metal chimneys

E6   A checklist for the visual inspection of a newly completed factory-made metal chimney is given in BS7566-3:1992 (1998), Section 10 and additional checks or particular variants may be included in manufacturers installation instructions. Following inspection, the chimney should be subjected to a smoke test.

Relined flues

E7   A flue which has been relined may be checked to show that it is free from restrictions, such as from surplus material (where that can occur) and that it is acceptably gastight by using the same tests as would be applied in the case of a newly built flue. However, a flue which has been relined with a flexible metal liner in accordance with Paragraph 3.36 of this Approved Document may be assumed to be unobstructed and acceptably gastight. (The use of a coring ball or inappropriate sweeps brushes can seriously damage a flexible metal flue liner.)

Appliances

E8   Where a combustion appliance is provided and connected up to the flue system as part of the work, the complete system of appliance and flue should be tested for gastightness in addition to testing the flue separately as above. For gas appliances an appropriate spillage test procedure is given in BS 5440-1:2000. For oil and solid fuel fired appliances suitable test procedures are given in BS 5410-1:1997 and BS 6461-1:1984 (1998) respectively.

Flue test procedures

Coring ball test

E9   This test may be appropriate for proving the minimum diameter of circular flues. It may also be used to check for obstructions in square flues but will not detect obstructions in the corners. (A purpose made coring ball or plate may need to be used if the flue is rectangular.) It is not applicable to fluepipes and should not be used with flexible metal flue liners. It should be carried out before smoke testing.

E10   A heavy ball, with a diameter about 25mm less than that of the flue, is lowered on a rope from the flue outlet to the bottom of the flue. If an obstruction is encountered, the blockage should be removed and the test repeated.

Smoke testing

E11   Where an existing flue is to be checked with a smoke test, it should first be swept.

E12   Two smoke testing procedures are described below. Test I confirms the gas-tightness of the whole flue and may be used for one serving a solid fuel or oil fired appliance or if there is any doubt over the condition of a gas flue. Test II may be used where the flue is to serve a gas fired appliance. Neither tests are substitutes for any spillage test required when commissioning the appliance. Other smoke testing procedures could be used where these form part of the procedure for the installation of an approved flue or relining system.

Smoke test I

E13   All doors and windows in the room served by the flue should be closed. The flue should first be warmed to establish a draught, e.g. with a blow lamp or electric heater. A suitable number of flue testing smoke pellets are placed at the base of the flue, such as in the fireplace recess or in the appliance if it is fitted, and ignited. When smoke starts to form, the base of the flue or fireplace opening should be sealed or the appliance should be closed, so that the smoke can only enter the flue. (For example, the recess opening should be closed off with a board or plate, sealed at the edges or, if the pellets are in the appliance, its doors, ashpit covers and vents should be closed).

E14   Smoke should be seen to issue freely from the flue outlet or terminal. When this is established, the top of the flue is sealed. The full length of the flue should then be checked, bearing in mind Paragraph E19, there should be no significant leakage. The test should be allowed to continue for at least 5 minutes. The closures at the top and bottom of the flue should then be removed.

Smoke test II

E15   All doors and windows in the room served by the flue should be closed. The flue should first be warmed to establish a draught. A suitable flue testing smoke pellet is ignited at the base of the flue or in the intended position of the appliance, so that the smoke is drawn into the flue with the rising draught. (If the pellets are placed in a recess at the base of the flue, the opening between the room and the recess should be partially closed, such as with a board, but so as to leave an air entry gap of about 25mm at the bottom).

E16   Smoke should be seen to issue freely from the flue outlet or terminal and not to spill back into the room. There should be no significant leakage of smoke from the length of the chimney inside or outside of the building.

E17   Smoke tests I and II are in line with the recommendations in BS 6461-1:1984 (1998) and BS 5440-1:2000.

Notes in relation to testing

E18   Where warming of the flue is specified, this is intended to establish a draught, but this may take more than 10 minutes in the case of large or cold flues.

E19   Appliances, where fitted, should not be under fire at the time of carrying out the test. During a smoke test, smoke should not emerge from the outlet of any other flue, as this indicates leakage between flues. When checking for smoke leakage from a flue, it should be borne in mind that smoke from a faulty flue can emerge some distance away from the original fault. In such cases, the smoke could emerge from such places as barge overhangs in end of terrace dwellings or from window reveals in cavity walls.

E20   The purpose of carrying out smoke testing is to check that flue gases will rise freely through the flue and to identify whether there are any faults, such as incorrectly sealed joints or damage that would cause the flue gases to escape into the dwelling.

E21   It should be noted that smoke pellets create a pressure significantly higher than the pressure required in the product standards for natural draught chimneys and for flues having a gas-tightness designation of N1. Flues to this designation are permitted to have a leakage rate of up to 2 litre/s/m² flue wall area. Some smoke leakage may therefore be seen during smoke tests and it can be a matter of expert judgement of whether leakage indicates failure.

E22   However, wisps of smoke visible on the outside of the chimney or near joints between chimney sections do not necessarily indicate a fault. If forceful plumes, or large volumes of smoke are seen, this could indicate a major fault such as an incorrectly made connection or joint, or a damaged section of chimney that requires investigation and remedial action followed by a repeat of the test.

Appendix F

ADDRESSES

ACE (Amalgamated Chimney Engineers): White Acre, Metheringham Fen, Lincoln LN4 3AL

Tel 01526 32 30 09 Fax01526 32 31 81

BFCMA (British Flue and Chimney Manufacturers Association): Henley Road, Medmenham, Marlow, Bucks SL7 2ER

Tel 01491 57 86 74   Fax 01491 57 50 24
info@feta.co.uk   www.feta.co.uk

BRE (Building Research Establishment Ltd.): Bucknalls Lane, Garston, Watford, Hertfordshire WD25 9XX

Tel 01923 66 4000   Fax 01923 66 4010
enquiries@bre.co.uk www.bre.co.uk

BSI (British Standards Institution): 389 Chiswick High Road, London W4 4AL

Tel 020 8996 9000   Fax 020 8996 7400
www.bsi-global.com

CIBSE (Chartered Institution of Building Services Engineers): 222 Balham High Road, London SW12 9BS

Tel 020 8675 5211   Fax 020 8675 5449
www.cibse.org

CORGI (The Council for Registered Gas Installers): 1, Elmwood, Chineham Business Park, Crockford Lane, Basingstoke, Hampshire RG24 8WG

Tel 01256 37 22 00   Fax 01256 70 81 44
www.corgi-gas.com

Environment Agency: Rio house, Waterside Drive, Aztec West, Almondsbury, Bristol BS32 4UD

Tel 0845 9333111   Fax 01454 624 409
www.environment-agency.gov.uk

(Publication enquiries to: Tel 01454 624 411   Fax 01454 624 014)

Environment Agency Emergency Hotline 0800 80 70 60

HETAS (Heating Equipment Testing and Approval Scheme): PO Box 37, Bishops Cleeve, Gloucestershire, GL52 4TB.

Tel 01242 673257   Fax 01242 673463
www.hetas.co.uk

HSE (Health and Safety Executive): Rose Court, 2 Southwark Bridge, London SE1 9HS

Tel 020 7717 6000   Fax 020 7717 6717
www.hse.gov.uk]

Gas safety advice line 0800 300 363

IGasE (Institution of Gas Engineers): 21 Portland Place, London W1B 1PY.

Tel 020 7636 6603   Fax 020 7636 6602
www.igaseng.com

LP Gas Association:
Pavilion 16, Headlands Business Park, Salisbury Road, Ringwood, Hampshire BH24 3PB.

Tel 01425 461612   Fax 01425 471131
www.lpga.co.uk

NACE (National Association of Chimney Engineers): PO Box 5666, Belper, Derbyshire, DE56 0YX

Tel 01773 599095   Fax 01773 599195
www.nace.org.uk

NACS (National Association of Chimney Sweeps): Unit 15, Emerald Way, Stone Business Park, Stone, Staffordshire, ST15 0SR

Tel 01785 811732 Fax 01785 811712
nacs@chimneyworks.co.uk
www.chimneyworks.co.uk

NFA (National Fireplace Association): 6th Floor, McLaren Building, 35 Dale End, Birmingham B4 7LN

Tel 0121 200 13 10   Fax 0121 200 13 06
www.nationalfireplaceassociation.org.uk

OFTEC (Oil Firing Technical Association for the Petroleum Industry): Century House, 100 High Street, Banstead, Surrey, SM7 2NN.

Tel 01737 37 33 11   Fax 01737 37 35 53
enquiries@oftec.org   www.oftec.org

SFA (Solid Fuel Association): 7 Swanwick Court, Alfreton, Derbyshire, DE55 7AS

Tel 0800 600 000   Fax 01773 834 351
sfa@solidfuel.co.uk   www.solidfuel.co.uk

Standards referred to

BS 41: 1973 (1981) Specification for cast Iron Spigot and Socket Flue or Smoke Pipes and Fittings.

BS 65: 1991 Specification for Vitrified Clay Pipes, Fittings and Ducts, Also Flexible Mechanical Joints for Use Solely with Surface Water Pipes and Fittings, AMD 8622.

BS EN 303-1: 1999 Heating Boilers. Heating Boilers with Forced Draught Burners. Terminology General Requirements, Testing and Marketing.

BS 476: Fire Tests on Building Materials and Structures, Part 4: 1970 (1984) Non-combustibility Test for Materials AMD 2483 and AMD 4390; Part 11: 1982 (1988) Method for Assessing the Heat Emission from Building Materials.

BS EN 449: 1997 Specification for Dedicated Liquified Petroleum Gas Appliances. Domestic Flueless Space Heaters (Including Diffusive Catalytic Combustion Heaters).

BS 715: 1993 Specification for Metal Flue Pipes, Fittings, Terminals and Accessories for Gas-Fired Appliances with a Rated Input Not Exceeding 60kW, AMD 8413.

BS 799: Oil Burning Equipment, Part 5: 1987 Specification for Oil Storage Tanks.

BS 1181: 1999 Specification for Clay Flue Linings and Flue Terminals.

BS 1251: 1987 Specification for Open Fireplace Components.

BS 1289-1: 1986 Flue Blocks and Masonry Terminals for Gas Appliances, Part 1: 1986 Specification for Precast Concrete Flue Blocks and Terminals; Part 2: 1989 Specification for Clay Flue Blocks and Terminals.

BS EN 1443: 1999 Chimneys. General Requirements.

BS 1449: Steel Plate, Sheet and Strip, Part 2: 1983 Specification for Stainless and Heat-Resisting Steel Plate, Sheet and Strip, AMD 4807, AMD 6646 and AMD 8828.

BS 1449-1: 1991 Steel plate, sheet and strip. Carbon and carbon manganese plate, sheet and strip. General specifications.

BS EN 1457: 1999 Chimneys. Clay/Ceramic Flue Liners. Requirements and Test Methods.

BS EN 1806: 2000 Chimneys. Clay/Ceramic Flue Blocks for Single Wall Chimneys. Requirements and Test Methods.

BS 1846: Glossary of Terms Relating to Solid Fuel Burning Equipment, Part 1: 1994 Domestic Appliances.

prEN 1857: 1995 Chimneys-Components-Concrete Flue Liners.

BS EN 1859:2000 Chimneys. Metal Chimneys. Test Methods.

BS 2869: 1998 Fuel Oils for Non-Marine Use, Part 2: 1988 Specification for Fuel Oil for Agricultural and Industrial Engines and Burners (Classes A2,C1, C2,D,E,F,G and H), AMD 6505.

BS 4543: Factory-Made Insulated Chimneys, Part 1: 1990 (1996) Methods of Test, AMD 8379; Part 2: 1990 (1996) Specification for Chimneys with Stainless Steel Flue Linings for Use with Solid Fuel Fired Appliances, AMD 8380; Part 3: 1990 (1996) Specification for Chimneys with Stainless Steel Fluelining for Use with Oil Fired Appliances, AMD 8381.

BS 4876: 1984 Specification for Performance Requirements for Domestic Flued Oil Burning Appliances (Including Test Procedures).

BS 5410: Code of Practice for Oil Firing, Part 1: 1977 Installations up to 44kW Output Capacity for Space Heating and Hot Water Supply Purposes, AMD 3637; Part 2: 1978 Installations of 44kW or Above Output Capacity for Space Heating, Hot Water and Steam Supply Purposes, AMD 3638.

BS 5440: Installation and Maintenance of Flues and Ventilation for Gas Appliances of Rated Input not exceeding 70Kw net (1st, 2nd and 3rd Family Gases), Part 1: 2000 Specification for Installation and maintenance of Flues; Part 2: 2000 Specification for Installation and Maintenance of Ventilation for Gas Appliances.

BS 5546: 2000 Specification for Installation of Hot Water Supplies for Domestic Purposes, Using Gas Fired Appliances of Rated Input not Exceeding 70Kw.

BS 5854: 1980 (1996) Code of Practice for Flues and Flue Structures in Buildings.

BS 5864: 1989 Specification for Installation in Domestic Premises of Gas-Fired Ducted-Air Heaters of Rated Input Not Exceeding 60kW, AMD 8130.

BS 5871: Specification for Installation of Gas Fires, Convector Heaters, Fire/Back Boilers and Decorative Fuel Effect Gas Appliances, Part 1: 2001 Gas Fires, Convector Heaters and Fire/Back Boilers and heating stoves (1st, 2nd and 3rd Family Gases); Part 2: 2001 Inset Live Fuel Effect Gas Fires of Heat Input Not Exceeding 15kW (2nd and 3rd Family Gases); Part 3: 2001 Decorative Fuel Effect Gas Appliances of Heat Input Not Exceeding 20kW (2nd and 3rd Family Gases), AMD 7033.

BS 6172: 1990 Specification for Installation of Domestic Gas Cooking Appliances (1st, 2nd and 3rd Family Gases).

BS 6173: 2001 Specification for Installation of Gas Fired Catering Appliances for Use in All Types of Catering Establishments (1st, 2nd and 3rd Family Gases).

BS 6461: Installation of Chimneys and Flues for Domestic Appliances Burning Solid Fuel (Including Wood and Peat), Part 1: 1984 (1998) Code of Practice for Masonry Chimneys and Flue Pipes.

BS 6798: 2000 Specification for Installation of Gas-Fired Boilers of Rated Input Not Exceeding 70kW.

BS 6999: 1989 (1996) Specification for Vitreous-Enamelled Low-Carbon-Steel Fluepipes, Other Components and Accessories for Solid-Fuel-Burning Appliances with a Maximum Rated Output of 45kW.

BS 7435: Fibre Cement Flue Pipes, Fittings and Terminals, Part 1: 1991 (1998) Specification for Light Quality Fibre Cement Flue pipes, Fittings and Terminals. Specifications for heavy quality cement flue pipes, fittings and terminals: Part 2 1991.

BS 7566: Installation of Factory-Made Chimneys to BS 4543 for Domestic Appliances, Part 1: 1992 (1998) Method of Specifying Installation Design Information; Part 2: 1992 (1998) Specification for Installation Design; Part 3: 1992 Specification for Site Installation; Part 4: 1992 (1998) Recommendations for Installation Design and Installation.

BS 8303: Installation of Domestic Heating and Cooking Appliances Burning Solid Mineral Fuels, Part 1: 1994 Specification for the Design of Installations; Part 2: 1994 Specification for Installing and Commissioning on Site; Part 3: 1994 Recommendations for Design and on Site Installation.

BS EN 10 088-1: 1995 Stainless Steels. List of Stainless Steels.

Other publications referred to

Approved Document J 2002: Supplementary Guidence on the UK Implementation of European Standards for Chimneys and Flues.

BRE Publications

BRE Report BR 414 (2001) Protective measures for housing on gas contaminated land ISBN 1 86081460 3

Radon: guidance on protective measures for new dwellings BR 211 (1999) Radon: guidance on protective measures for new dwellings. ISBN 1 86081 3283

Good Building Guide 25 Radon and Buildings (1996) ISBN 1 86081 0705

Spillage of flue gases from solid-fuel combustion appliances. BRE IP 7/94.

CIBSE Design Guide

Volume B Installation and Equipment Data.

Environment Agency pollution prevention publications

The Control of Polution (Oil Storage) (England) Regulations (2001).

Pollution Prevention Guidelines PPG2 - Above Ground Oil Storage Tanks.

Masonry Bunds for Oils Storage Tanks

Concrete Bunds for Oils Storage Tanks

Above documents available without charge from DMS Mailing House:

Fax 0151 604 1222;
email environment-agency@dmsltd.co.uk

Health and Safety Executive

Safety in the installation and use of gas systems and appliances, Approved Code of Practice and Guidance L56. HSE Books ISBN 0 7176 1635 5.

The Gas Safety (Installations and Use) Regulations 1998

Gas Appliances (Safety) Regulations 1995.

Workplace, Safety and Welfare, Workplace (Health, Safety and Welfare) Regulations 1992. Approved Code of Practice L24. HSE Books, 1992 ISBN 0 7176 0413 6.

LP Gas Association

Code of Practice 1 Bulk LPG Storage at Fixed Installations Part1:1998, Design, Installation and Operation of Vessels Located Above Ground.

OFTEC Publications

OFTEC Oil Fired Appliance Standard. OFS A100. Heating Boilers with Atomising Burners. Outputs up to 70kW. Maximum Operating Pressures of 3 Bar.

OFTEC Oil Fired Appliance Standard. OFS A101. Oil Fired Cookers with Atomising or Vaporising Burners with or without Boilers. Heat Outputs up to 45kW.

TI/112 Oil Firing Industry Technical Advice. Oil Fired Appliances and Extract Fans.

Your Garden Walls. Better to be Safe than Sorry

Product code 91 HCN 0227.
Available from: DTLR Free Literature, PO Box 236, Wetherby, West Yorkshire, LS23 7NB

Tel 0870 1226236   Fax 0870 1226237
Textphone 0870 1207405
Email dtlr@twoten.press.net